Fart Sounds:

The reason(s) why
Jokes are funny

From the writers, producers, directors and performers of: Bob's Burgers, Cartoon Network, Comedy Central, The Comedy Store, The Comedy Cellar, The Daily Show, Full Frontal, GIRLS, Hollywood Improv, Inside Amy Schumer, IFC, Jimmy Kimmel Live!, The Knitting Factory, The Late Show, The Laugh Factory, Last Comic Standing, Last Week Tonight, Maron, @midnight, MADtv, MTV, The New York Times, Second City, UCB, VICELAND, and more.

Curated by Zuri Irvin

DEDICATION

I'd like to thank my mom, Jackie, and dad, Robert, for literally making all of this happen. And to my brother, Chad, and sister, Mali, thanks for laughing.

To Coltrane, welcome to the world!

And thank *you* for buying this book

TABLE OF CONTENTS

*Please note that people
often fit into multiple categories
**There's also an index
at the back of the book

INTRO

You're probably reading this and thinking: 'Who the hell is this guy?' or 'What's Amazon's return policy?'

And I can't really blame you. This was a huge risk on your part. Plus, you're probably already funny. But since you've already paid for this, and are reading it now, let's at least get comfortable with the idea that we're in this together. We both love comedy and we probably both value laughter in a weird way. This collection is designed to explore reasons why comedians become comedians and what makes jokes funny.

I've been lucky enough to engage with some of the most talented, unique and helpful people in the business; who all helped put this together without asking for anything in return. I think that illustrates the selflessness of comedy. And also why it's so hard to make money in this industry.

Anyways, blah, blah, blah. Please enjoy and just know that you're already really cool for reading this.

LATE NIGHT TV

J.R. HAVLAN

🐦 @JRHavlan

J.R. moved to New York in 1988 to begin his stand-up career and thanks to hard work, dedication and hustle, he soon found work as a waiter. Some years after that he performed stand-up on The Late Show with David Letterman and Late Night with Conan O'Brien as well as making numerous other television appearances that didn't matter nearly as much. In 1996, J.R. became a writer on The Daily Show. In 1999, it became The Daily Show with Jon Stewart and that's when the Emmys started pouring in thanks in small part to J.R. himself (Eight so far!).

Why did you first want to start performing comedy? What was the first joke or bit you tried on stage?

I was a wise-cracker in grammar school but mainly out of boredom. There were no conscious career choices happening for me back then, but I was definitely drawn to comedy. The $1 theater in my town was playing Woody Allen's "Take the Money and Run" when I was 13 and I went to see it 28 times. To this day, I carry a slice of bologna in my wallet in the event things go south and I have to share it with my family. *

Between that movie and the books "Without Feathers" and "Getting Even" I couldn't think of anything else I wanted to do more than make people laugh. I didn't start performing stand-up until I moved to New York City in 1988. I don't recall my first joke, but it was probably something about how dirty the subway was or what a hassle it was when you had to make a phone call but you didn't have a dime on you. What a hassle!! Right, kids?

(*May or may not be true)

Where did you grow up?

I grew up in a suburb of San Francisco, California, called Danville, which is now a fairly ritzy town, but back in the '70s was filled with bell-bottomed kids standing around a keg in a field listening to ZZ Top blasting out of a low-end car stereo.

What's interesting or uninteresting about Danville?

Interesting question. Though I didn't realize this at the time, what was interesting and uninteresting about Danville in the '70s is basically an almost completely overlapping Venn Diagram. We were bored, which sucked, so we'd ride our bikes to a construction site, get high, and shoot bottles with a BB gun, which was amazing. The only 'clubs' were the roller skating rink and the bowling alley, so we'd have our parents drop us off at one or the other, skate or bowl for an hour, and then sneak out and party for the rest of the night... in a field... with a keg... listening to ZZ Top... or maybe Aerosmith.

I also liked Aerosmith. Basically, if you've ever seen the movies "Dazed and Confused" or "Over The Edge" that's pretty much all you need to know to understand the place in which I grew up.

What did your parents do for a living when you were a kid?

They got divorced when I was ten. Thanks a lot for bringing it up! But my mom was a librarian at a high school, though not the one I went to; and my dad was always self-employed—mainly with a landscaping business that he owned and a bar that he owned that had a one-table lo-ball poker room in the back, was attached to a pool hall, and was across the street from a putt-putt golf park. That bar was one of my favorite places on earth. It was called "Johnny's" but that wasn't my dad's name.

Can you talk about how you started writing for Politically Incorrect and how that parlayed into a job with The Daily Show?

I stuck my foot in the door at P.I. by asking a friend who was a writer's assistant there if he could get me the fax number for submitting monologue jokes. He did that and I started faxing in jokes… on a fax machine. Let me explain. You see, a "fax machine" was sort of a… oh, forget it.

The important thing is, Bill started using a decent amount of my jokes and before I knew it, I was asked to join the writing staff for a three-week "trial." It didn't work out. I thought it was going great, and most of the rest of the writing staff thought so too, but it would seem we were all wrong. Turned out for the best, because I got the job on The Daily Show not long after I left P.I. That was basically unrelated, though. If you want a real break down of how I ended up at TDS, listen to my Writers' Bloc Podcast episode with Lizz Winstead who co-created TDS and was responsible for hiring me.

In a nutshell, I knew Lizz from stand-up and she asked me to submit for this new "shitty little show" she was putting together, so I did, and 18 years later I decided I'd had enough.

What are some of the things you enjoyed most about the creation process at The Daily Show?

That it was almost constantly evolving. The Daily Show was, and I'm sure still is, like a shark—if it didn't keep moving it would die. Also, it had a second row of teeth. Not a lot of people know that. It's a big industry secret.

The Daily Show was an amazing place. Even before Jon took over we knew we had something fun and special going on, but once Jon did arrive, it quickly became a phenomenon and somehow maintained that status for an obscene amount of time.

Most of that credit goes to Jon, of course, but one of his greatest talents was attracting, choosing and nurturing other great talent, both on-air and behind the scenes.

Unless you worked at The Daily Show, you could never fully understand how smoothly and effectively the staff was able to put together such great shows night after night. I was constantly amazed by it and thrilled to be a part of it. Plus, we got a free catered lunch every day. Top that!

How do you think Larry Wilmore and Trevor Noah are doing in their new roles? What types of pressures do they face?

Well, Larry's in a far different position than Trevor of course because he simply replaced an enormously successful existing show whereas Trevor had to take over an even more enormously successful existing show. Both jobs are hard, but one is considerably more of a public challenge. I know Larry, but I've only met Trevor a couple of times. Both men are extremely smart and talented and they have excellent shows that they do almost every night.

That's a very difficult task regardless of external pressure. Though I probably only actually watch each of the shows once or twice a week, I enjoy both of them very much. It's a little hard because they both remind me of something that was very special to me but is no longer a part of my life. It's sort of like watching an old girlfriend make out with some other guy. It's kind of a turn on until I realize, "Oh! Right! I used to be that guy!"

That's usually when I turn the channel.

What advice would you give someone who is trying to write for a late night comedy show?

Don't be discouraged by failure. The job you're trying to get is 98-percent failure, even once you get it. In other words, writing for a late night comedy show is a matter of churning out ridiculous amounts of very good material even though only very small amounts of extremely good material actually make it on to the show. So putting your best effort into something you're relatively certain will end up in the shredder is a huge part of the job.

As for the business side of it, you have to make connections. You have to become a part of the comedy community at any level and keep working your way up. Performing stand-up, improv, sketch, creating a web series—all of these things force you to continue writing and performing, but they also keep you in touch with the people who might one day hire you. Or better yet, the people you might hire. And one more thing, if there's a particular show that you find yourself drawn to, one that you feel best suited for, then write for that show even though you're not writing for that show. Always be working on your submission packet for that show even if you don't know what the submission packet looks like. Only by writing in someone else's voice every day will you be able to eventually capture that person's voice, and if you can do that you'll be far more prepared than most people when the opportunity hopefully comes to actually submit your material.

What was the inspiration behind the The Writers' Bloc Podcast?

The primary reason I do the podcast is to basically give something back to the comedy world. I've worked very hard, but I've also been very fortunate. It occurred to me that when I was trying to break into comedy writing I would love to have had the opportunity to hear from people who were already doing what I wanted to do.

The podcast is for the benefit of the so-called "BlocHeads" out there, many of whom have no other way to hear first-hand what it takes to become a comedy writer and what it's like once you actually get there. The additional benefit was that I got to meet a lot of people I respected and have long, meaningful conversations with them as well as with old friends. I mean, how often do you sit down and just talk to somebody one-on-one for an hour? Especially somebody you're not trying to have sex with. It's a pretty special thing.

Do you prefer forming jokes on paper or on stage?

I don't get on stage that much anymore, so most of what I do is on paper, by which I mean "in computer." These days I use paper exclusively to start fires, make little airplanes, and occasionally experiment with little flaming airplanes. When I was doing stand-up I loved writing it and I loved coming up with things on stage, but most of the stuff I came up with on stage was "in the moment" and I usually had a hard time ever turning those moments into recurring bits. It just never felt right to me. As hard as it is to do, I love sitting down and writing, but one thing I often do to stimulate the writing process is record ideas and often incoherent ramblings into my phone. Then I sit down at my computer and listen to those recordings. More often than not, that gets me started and as we all know, just getting started can be the hardest part of writing.

Is there a gap in televised news-comedy right now? Where is the genre headed?

I don't think there's a gap. If anything it's flooded, but in a good way, for now at least. Between Trevor, Larry, John Oliver, Bill Maher, Weekend Update and soon, Sam Bee, there are more than enough shows to help the public dissect the folly of our world in a funny way. It's actually the most crowded it's ever been, but that's the nature of entertainment at this point. There are so many outlets and there is so much talent, that there's finally room for (almost) everybody. That's both a good and a not-so-good thing in that we get the benefit of choosing who we want to have feed us our daily satire, but we might also get tired of it relatively soon. The trend now, led by Oliver in my opinion, is toward honest, purposeful comedy meant not only to entertain, but to truly inform and incite—in a good way. Not in a "set this town on fire" way. That would be bad, depending on the town. I love to have a simple laugh at some goofy bit of pointless comedy, but I prefer to laugh because I not only think something's funny, but I also think it's truly insightful and meaningful. It makes me feel less like I'm wasting my time.

Guatemala just elected a comedian with no political experience to be president. Do you think that could ever happen in the United States? Why or why not?

I am so perplexed by politics at this point that I wouldn't dare predict the future. The present political scene is already playing out like a screwball comedy. I think your real question is probably, "Will Jon ever run for office?" The answer is I have no idea and I think he probably wouldn't, though if he did, I suppose it wouldn't surprise me. The only surprise would be if he lost. I guess I'd also be surprised if the position he ran for was Alderman or Dog Catcher.

I prefer to believe he would reach a little higher than that.

What do you like or dislike about comedy in New York?

What I like is that there are thousands of "stages" and everybody has at least some opportunity to "show us what they've got." What I don't like is the same thing I never liked about comedy, business, life, high school, you name it—there are cliques that can often be self-serving sometimes at the expense of true talent. That's not to say the people in those cliques (and no, I can't name them because it's more of an "idea" than anything else) aren't talented, but there are times when opportunity can elude you simply because of who you know or don't know. And worse, judgement can be severely impaired by personal relationships. But hey, that's life. Deal with it, bitch!

Who is the funniest person you know?

Whoever's making me laugh at the moment. I don't have a top-ten list or anything like that. I have friends who are not in comedy but with whom I often share my biggest laughs. Of course, there are also stand outs like John Oliver, Stephen Colbert, Louis CK (if that is his real name), Sam Bee, Kate McKinnon on SNL makes me laugh the second any part of her body enters the frame. But there is no "funniest person." There's just the funniest person at any given moment, which is totally fine with me.

Oh! Wait! Me.

I think I was supposed to say "me." Argh! Too late!

Why are jokes funny?

For the same reason they're not funny—because that's what you think.

JENA FRIEDMAN

@JenaFriedman

Jena is a stand-up comedian, actor, writer and filmmaker. She has worked as a field producer at The Daily Show with Jon Stewart and has written for Late Show with David Letterman. When she's not on tour, she can be seen performing stand-up and improv at venues such as The Upright Citizen's Brigade Theater, The Stand and The Comedy Cellar.

Is there anything you can or can't talk about with The Daily Show?

Yeah, probably none of it. (laughs)

Ah, okay. Even generally speaking?

Generally speaking, it's awesome! I'm leaving, actually, today. Today's my last day. But the new iteration of the show is going to be great. This current show is the best job I've ever had. I put it all out on Twitter. This is a great, great place. There are really wonderful, smart, thoughtful people making comedy that says something. It's great.

How did you end up joining the show as a field producer?

So I had written for Letterman and I was doing stand-up and my friend Wyatt Cenac was actually the one who recommended me based on this web series that I made called Ted & Gracie. Anyways, the job of a field producer is writing and directing field segments. So I had stuff that I wrote and produced that I could show them and they called me in and I did a sample field piece and that's how I got the job.

When you're researching field pieces, how do you go about aggregating information and making sure you're prepared?

We have a whole team of people. We'll come up with stories— Jon's always encouraging of us doing stuff that we're passionate about. So if we find a story and there's a funny angle on it, we have associate producers help us book the elements together and make the phone calls.

One thing I didn't realize until I came here is that it's pretty much scripted before you go out. You pre-interview the politician to get a sense of what they're going to say, and then you sit down with them; but it's very, very planned out. And the people we talk to are all real people. We never take them out of context... it's all real stuff.

Do you have any experiences where you crossed the line or asked something you didn't want to ask?

No. (laughs)

What are you working on next?

I have a film that I wrote that I'm directing— we're just kind of assembling everything now. I'm in pre-production on a feature and am directing and developing a comedic show for truTV. And I have a show that I'm putting up in Scotland. It's like, a solo stand-up show that's going to be in the Edinburgh Film Festival in two weeks.

What is the show in Scotland about?

It's a stand up show called American Cunt, and it's basically my political comedy.

Have you ever thought about running for office?

Me? No. Never. I just like making fun of it.

So you'd rather stay in this side of it?

Yeah, there's no ... it never even ... that's the last thing I'd ever do. I think you can change the system more effectively, at least I can personally, from the outside of it.

What you do mean?

Right out of college I actually worked at a management consulting firm in health care in Chicago. I was very young and naive and actually knew that healthcare needed changing.

I thought: 'The best way to change the system is from within!' So, we would actually consult large health insurers and give them recommendations (how to better serve the community, cut healthcare costs, etc.) and it taught me how limited the changes are within a system.

And so that's when I realized I wanted to make fun of it.

Didn't you do a piece on Monsanto? And one on water contamination in West Virginia?

Yeah, Jon has been very cool about letting us do exactly what we want to do. I did a piece on the food worker's strikes, and a piece on fracking as well. One piece that I feel definitely had an impact was a piece I did with Aasif Mandvi on the voter ID laws in North Carolina ... I definitely feel like some of these pieces have been impactful in a wonderful way. Or, I hope they have. I could be biased.

How did you first start writing for Letterman?

I had been doing stand-up and I submitted a packet through a management company. And then a year later that management company, like, dropped me because I could never get a job (laughs). Letterman's people asked me to submit another packet. So I did and I got the job that day.

Oh, wow. Is that the norm for writers getting into late night?

I don't really know. Everyone has a different path. I never thought I'd be writing for late night but I remember doing stand-up in Chicago and coming to New York and seeing women I admired like Morgan Murphy, Chelsea Peretti and Jessi Klein. And they were all doing stand-up and writing on shows, so I thought, I guess I should be able to pay my rent. I should try to write on a show. I had a manager at the time and I started submitting sample packets, and submitting sample packets … so I remember submitting a Letterman packet and thinking it was *so* funny. I never had that confidence in a writing sample. And then a year later I heard from them and they wanted to see another sample. So I got it to them the next morning and I ended up with the job.

Do you ever go back to Chicago to do stand-up?

Not enough! My family is actually from outside of Philly. I don't go back to Chicago enough. I was there with The Daily Show Live Tour doing stand-up, but I don't really go back there as much as I'd like. It's a great place to do comedy.

Does that make you a Phillies fan or a Cubs fan?

Uh…

Or Neither?

Uh, I don't know. That's baseball, right? (laughs)

What makes a joke funny?

Pot? Pot makes jokes funny.

MILES KAHN

🐦 *@mileskahn*

Miles is an award-winning filmmaker currently working as Executive Producer for Full Frontal with Samantha Bee on TBS. He previously served as Senior Producer for The Daily Show with Jon Stewart on Comedy Central, and Executive Producer for DL Hughley: The Endangered List, which was honored with a 2013 Peabody Award. He seeks your love and approval.

Is there anything you learned in film school that you still use on shoots today?

There's a ton that I learned that still applies. When I started as a PA it was no different than PA'ing in New York. Just bigger budgets. But it's the intangibles—"hurry up and wait," and understanding how the chain of command works. I've hopefully gotten better at directing, though.

What inspired Fly Trap?

I really wanted to do a simply-told comedy. The whole story just came to me one afternoon. I wrote it down and wrote the story in 15 minutes. It came from me being a lonely sap in Astoria and watching my Latino neighbors run around having a good time. Also, I worked in my love of Chubby Hubby ice cream.

My college thesis was really complex and in some ways overwrought with plots and themes. I'm glad I made mistakes on that as I feel like I corrected them with Fly Trap.

What was your first project that you were really proud of and why?

At the time, getting a job at The Daily Show certainly made me proud. I put in a lot of hours before then on shows I didn't always love and I had admired Jon and his crew for so long. But I have to say that being able to create something new with Samantha Bee at Full Frontal is equally as amazing.

But really my first break was a gig to develop a show for MTV. I'd never gotten paid as a director so while I had no interest in reality TV, I jumped at the chance to do something where I'd finally have the "director" title. That show turned into MTV's Room Raiders. It's not great TV, but it was the longest running strip show in MTV history.

It made money for the bosses. It was a terrible gig; really punishing. But you learn more on the bad ones. I learned a lot.

You produced a ton of tremendous pieces with The Daily Show. What are some creative skills you picked up while working there?

Collaboration and the meritocracy of ideas. I came out of film school maybe a bit of a snob. My vision was paramount to any project. TDS put me in a room with super smart and funny people and the best joke would win. Didn't matter who came up with it. Now, I prefer working in groups over the more "artiste" route. Jon pushed us all to challenge ourselves to find the better joke. Throw the first one away. You can do better. That was important.

I've heard that Jon Stewart often asked correspondents to have their own, distinct opinions on things. Is that part of what makes for good material?

The more the talent is invested in the take and story, the better. Certainly.

What is the origin story behind Halal in the Family?

Katie Couric once commented that what Muslims needed was a "Cosby Show" of their own. So Aasif Mandvi and I took that idea and made it into a TDS piece called the "Qu'osby Show"—a terrible sitcom about a Muslim dad trying too hard to fit in. We loved shooting it. Years later he and his manager and producer, Lillian LaSalle, approached me about making it a web series. We reinvented it a bit as "Halal in the Family" and did our best to avoid any connection to Cosby (the TDS piece was shot before we discovered what a criminally awful douche he was).

How do you guys choose which subjects to tackle on Full Frontal?

If it makes us angry or outraged or laugh or cry. We challenge ourselves to find stories that don't have a natural comedy angle. It makes our job super hard. But doing stories about abortion and Syrian refugees has proven to be HILARIOUS. OK, maybe not that, but we like what we're doing.

What advice would you give someone who wants work in late night?

Get out there and make stuff. Shoot stuff, write stuff, meet people, do improv. Do everything.

Why do you think comedians become comedians?

They're incredibly sad people.

What makes a joke funny?

I'm still figuring that one out.

My grandpa told terrible Borscht Belt jokes. I still love them. I go from the Marx brothers to Patton Oswalt and back.

JOSH GONDELMAN

🐦 @joshgondelman

Josh is a writer and comedian who incubated in Boston before moving to New York City, where he currently lives and works as a writer for Last Week Tonight with John Oliver. This spring, he made his late night stand-up debut on Conan (TBS), and he can also be seen on the first season of Night Train With Wyatt Cenac (SeeSo). Josh's newest comedy album Physical Whisper debuted in March at #1 on the iTunes comedy charts (as well as #4 on the Billboard comedy chart) and stayed there for...well...longer than he expected, honestly.

Where did you grow up?

I grew up in Stoneham, a little suburb of Boston. It's pronounced "Stone 'em" because Massachusetts doesn't bend to the will of "how letters are supposed to be said."

What's interesting or uninteresting about Stoneham?

Growing up there was great. It's kind of like the Massachusetts version of a town in a Bruce Springsteen song, which, I think if The Boss were being honest, he'd admit were perfectly nice places to grow up. Although, there are lots of car accidents along the side of the highway in his songs. The police in New Jersey really needed to crack down on drunk driving; then these towns would have been way more hospitable. My town was like that! Nothing too exciting, but full of nice people. Nancy

Kerrigan, the figure skater, is from there. And there's a zoo that used to have a polar bear.

What did your parents do for a living when you were a kid?

My mom was a teacher and then later the director of a small private school. My dad was a glazier (he installed glass and aluminum storefronts/windows). They're super great and supportive! They're both retired now, and they spend a lot of time taking walks and seeing live music. My parents go to so many shows! They're like the retired version of like… scene kids, or whatever kids who see a lot of shows are called now!

Why did you first want to start performing comedy? What was the first joke or bit you tried on stage?

I just loved jokes so much as a child. I remember wanting to perform at like…age seven by reading from a kids' joke book, and my parents being like: "That's not what stand-up comedy is," and me being like: "Not yet it isn't! I'm going to change the game."

The first bit I ever tried (in my late teens, probably) was very Seinfeld-y. It was about places that sold medium and large sizes with no small, and how that's just not okay.

Modern Seinfeld is one of Twitter's most unique conceptions. What is the story behind its creation?

Well thanks! I appreciate your compliment but it is based pretty heavily on some existing stuff. Namely…actual Seinfeld. I remember a conversation with my friend Dan Boulger, who's an incredibly funny comedian from Boston, and he said that if there were cell phones, you'd lose half the episodes of Seinfeld. And I was thinking, no, you'd gain a million new ones! So I started tweeting plot lines from my own account, and my friend Jack Moore started playing along and snatched up the 🐦 *@SeinfeldToday* handle, and we started writing them together.

When did you realize it was going to be enormously popular?

Not at all! I think when I started tweeting from my own account, and people latched on I was like: "Oh neat! This is a fun game!" But Jack very astutely realized that it could have a longer life. I never assume anyone will see or like things I do, honestly!

What inspired You Blew It!? What kind of person should go out and buy your book?

Joe (Berkowitz, my co-author) and I had pitched a fake pickup artist guide called Getting It Wet: The Nice Guy's Guide To Tricking Women From Friendzone To Bonezone, and no one wanted to buy it. But! We met an editor who liked our stuff and helped us fit our voices into something less viscerally objectionable to people! So it was born out of a desire to point out what kinds of people/places/things are nightmares.

It's perfect for people whose lives are generally good but who are still flustered by the finer points of living in the world. Or if you think the Earth is an irredeemable garbage barge floating through space…you'll also probably like it.

What advice would you give a young comedian?

Oh gosh! My general advice for writers/comedians is: Make stuff you like and are proud of. Put it in a place where people can see it, whether that's onstage or on the internet or wherever. Just do the things that make you happy creatively, and then show them to people. Plus, be nice to people and make friends whose work you admire and who like your stuff too. Most other advice I'd give is just a variant of those three things.

Last Week Tonight has really broken ground on how cable news is reported. How did you start writing for the show?

Well, I think I'd be remiss if I didn't point out that I'm just a comedy writer working for a comedy show! I applied by submitting a sample set of materials when they were picking the original writing staff. I got hired to do all their digital content last year, and this year I moved over to write more for the show itself. My favorite thing is how everyone in the office is so talented but also so friendly and kind. All of my bosses are wonderful. Plus, the writers are all so, so funny and great to work with. And that's true all the way through the office from the editors to the research staff to the producers in the field.

What do you like or dislike about comedy in New York?

I like how many amazing comedians there are to watch on any given night. I like eating pizza while walking between shows. I like that the trains run all night. Also, there is an underrated camaraderie among comedians, and it's not as cutthroat as people make it out to be. That's true lots of places, but in New York it was more of a surprise to me because of the city's reputation.

Who is the funniest person you know?

Oh boy. I get to be around professionally funny people all the time, but maybe the hardest I've laughed each of the past three years was driving home to Massachusetts for Thanksgiving with my old roommates (comedian) Sean Wilkinson and (writer) Jason Marcus and just doing four hours of characters and riffs. Both of those guys are so talented as writers/performers, but we spent so much time together just hanging out when we lived together that I've spent longer laughing at them than any other people.

Why are jokes funny?

One of my college professors (the excellent Dr. Caren Irr) said that a joke gives people the pleasure of having an idea without doing the work of thinking, and I love that definition.

But also, in my experience, jokes are funny because of yelling in a Boston accent or making up silly-sounding words.

JILL TWISS

Jill is also a staff writer on HBO's Last Week Tonight with John Oliver. She is an actress, singer and comedian in New York City.

Where did you grow up?

I grew up all over. I was born in Redmond, Oregon and then moved to Utah, Idaho, Montana, back to a different place in Idaho, back to a different place in Oregon, Minnesota and Virginia. That was all before college.

I went to 11 schools in 12 years. To the best of my knowledge, we were not running from the law.

Generally speaking, what are some things you've learned about comedy writing since joining Last Week Tonight?

I've learned that you can write an infinite number of jokes on a topic, so don't get too precious with your own work. When I started, I would think "I did it! I found the joke!" as though it were some sort of secret buried treasure—and if I found it, then I won and was finished searching**. And then, of course, it would be cut for any one of a zillion completely great reasons and I would be devastated. Jokes, it turns out, are an entirely renewable resource and I can always make more of them and it really makes my day go by a lot easier if I remember that.

**Incidentally, as a child I also thought this was true with Easter egg hunts. My parents were never able to get across to me that there was more than one egg hidden, and that finding a single egg and screaming "I WON" did not mean I had, in fact, "won" the Easter egg hunt.

What advice would you give someone who wants to write for a late night show?

Write jokes every day. Like, a lot of them. More than you think. Lots of people watch a TV show and think "I could do that." I get it. I think that when I watch the luge in the Olympics. (I am objectively wrong about this.)

But if you actually want to write comedy for a living, you have to write jokes constantly. And then you will get better at it. I used to sit and write jokes for two hours every day well before I had anywhere to submit those jokes. Then when someday you have the chance to submit jokes for a late night show, presto, you will already have a lot of jokes! More importantly, you will be able to write jokes on command, something that is exponentially harder than writing jokes when something inspires you—and something that is really important when comedy is your job.

Why do you think comedians become comedians?

I think one thing most comedians have in mind is feeling like an outsider—which by the way, isn't a bad thing. Outside is the best place to observe. And it's hard to see society's quirks when you're in the middle of them.

What would you be doing if you weren't working in comedy?

I wasn't working in comedy for most of my life. I was doing theatre, singing, auditioning, tutoring SATs and LSATs, waiting tables, and...writing comedy. If I weren't working in comedy, I would still be writing comedy. Just no one would be saying it out loud on a television show and my grocery lists would be super witty.

What makes a joke funny?

It helps if it has penguins. You're welcome.

Also funny jokes, I think, are this weird Venn Diagram with an overlap between "References The Audience Understands" and "Things The Audience Hasn't Thought Of Yet." If no one gets the reference then it's not funny. And if everyone gets the reference and made exactly the same observation you did, then it's not funny. So it's a very tiny overlap of "Thoughts I Understand Yet Have Not Had Yet." Oh my god I just read what I wrote and it is the least funny thing anyone has ever said.

New advice: To be funny, do whatever the opposite of whatever I just did in that last paragraph. Penguins.

CORY CAVIN

🐦 *@corycavin*

Cory is a comedian, writer, and producer in New York City. He was the head blogger for Late Night with Jimmy Fallon where he received two Emmy Awards and three Emmy nominations for Outstanding Creative Achievement In Interactive Media. He made videos for VH1's Best Week Ever blog, was a producer for Nikki & Sara Live on MTV and has written for MTV and Nickelodeon. He hosts the NYC stand up show Great Times with Cory + Kevin and is part of the comedy group Awful DJ, which was nominated for a WGA Award for their series Model Wife.

When did you first realize you could write and perform for a living?

After college I wanted to be a video editor for a living but I always had this dream of "going to New York to do improv." I didn't really know what that meant, I just knew there were theaters there where you could be on stage and be funny doing improv. I knew you could make a living working in TV & film because that was my major in college.

After I decided to finally move to New York to get involved at UCB doing improv, I started taking jobs in TV production because that was my background, both from school and from working as an assistant on TV commercials back in North Carolina. Slowly I learned what writers and producers did on TV shows and how actors booked jobs and I started to realize I wanted to work in comedy and make a living doing it. I also learned how much I hated my NYC temp job outside of entertainment so working in comedy seemed like a much better option.

What's interesting or uninteresting about Charlotte?

Charlotte was always a real city, not a tiny town, but I never thought anyone had ever heard of it because it seemed small. Now that I've been away from there for about 10 years, I've realized it's grown a lot and is a major city. I never knew how to describe Charlotte when I was growing up there because it never had a very defined identity as a city. Then I moved to New York City and realized Charlotte is very nice and clean (especially in comparison to how dirty NYC is). I love New York but it is kinda filthy compared to Charlotte; my clean childhood home.

What did you parents do for a living when you were a kid?

My mom was an elementary school teacher assistant and my dad was a hardware salesman.

How did you start making videos for VH1's Best Week Ever blog?

I interned with a friend at the UCB Theatre and eventually I lived with him and his roommates, and they both worked at the TV show Best Week Ever. At the time I worked as an associate producer and assistant editor on a reality show about big extravagant weddings and the brides that planned them. By the time that job ended I was in a different apartment but I called my old roommates and they told me Best Week Ever needed an editor to work overnight and make a video podcast called Best Night Ever.

I sent in my resume, had an interview, and ended up doing that job for two years. It really messed up my sleep schedule but it was so much fun and I got to work with great people who are now doing amazing things in comedy.

What was your creation process at Late Night with Jimmy Fallon?
Why do you think his show(s) work so well?

The process changed over time because the internet changed over time. When I started there, Twitter was barely big and Instagram hadn't even been invented yet. Our process was always to make high quality content in Jimmy's voice and find cool ways to do things. Jimmy loves to keep things positive so that always played into the creation process. Also since Jimmy loved to see "cool" things and not just comedic things, that let us think outside of the traditional formats for making comedy.

So we tried to pitch different, innovative ways to show off fun things happening at the show. We could do more than just web sketches or write internet lists. It opened up a lot of fun possibilities. I got to make a web series called Late Night Eats were famous chefs made cheap high quality meals and we even got Nick Offerman to come on and make a recipe his character Ron Swanson would make. It freed us up to make music videos with the bands when they were backstage. We made a backstage video tour that played out like a Choose Your Own Adventure game on YouTube. We wrote product reviews of weird free stuff that companies sent to the Late Night offices. We did a photo essay of Paul Scheer touring the NBC Commissary. We got normal moms and dads from the audience to have their pictures taken with Gwar.

When Late Night first started we looked at the show like Jimmy was hosting a big party, so we wanted to find ways to reach out to the audience and let them get in on bits. When Twitter became popular bits like "Hashtags" emerged as a way for Jimmy to make jokes with his audience on a broad scale. We took fan questions from Tumblr. Jimmy used Skype questions from fans in interviews. I think the show works well because a fan really feels included, like you're part of that party what Jimmy is hosting. You're getting to see cool things happen and you can even have a voice in the show.

Model Wife is delightfully written and keeps a stellar pace. How did you come up with the idea for the series?

Thanks! The idea came when my comedy group Awful DJ (myself, Josh Lay, and Bill Grandberg) wanted to make a series. We took a while figuring it out. We all threw out different ideas for series when we were on a retreat in North Carolina at my parents' house. We had a bunch of ideas. One of them was a series idea I wanted to make on my own where I had a beautiful supermodel girlfriend and every episode would be a short awkward interaction between her and I. Just dumb little 30 second episodes like me making a giant dinner and when I fill my plate, she eats three pieces of lettuce and is full. High quality hilarity like that.

From there we took it and worked it out. One day Josh and I were running errands driving a van around NYC and ended up driving a few hours thinking how to make it bigger and better. Bill and I talked about it when we were on a trip in upstate NY where he grew up. All three of us marinated on ideas for a while and eventually we came up with Model Wife and wrote three pilot scripts. We shot them all in a weekend and those became the first three episodes. I'm so glad we grew it bigger from the original little idea because it is one of the most fun and well done things we've ever made.

How did you and Kevin James Doyle first get together to form GREAT TIMES!?

Kevin and I were "set up on a comedy date" by mutual friends. Mutual friends told me I should meet him because he did stand-up and they told him they had another friend that did comedy and at the time worked at Late Night with Jimmy Fallon. Our mutual friend would routinely text me bad jokes and ask me to pitch them to Jimmy for the show.

I went to see Kevin perform and after we made plans to hang out and go to an open mic together. After that open mic Kevin and I stood awkwardly on the street like you do after a real first date and we talked about staying in touch. Just two nervous straight dudes wanting to get in a comedy relationship with each other. Eventually we became better friends and started more stand-up together. Kevin wanted to start a show and asked if I wanted to co-host with him (finally! He noticed me!). Then we found our venue and started hosting the show in January 2014 and it's been great.

Do you prefer forming jokes on paper or on stage? Why?

I prefer doing it onstage. I'm a pretty social person so in my best moments I can take an idea I think is funny and riff on it in front of any audience and find what's funny there and what's natural for me. Then I can take what worked and write it down and try it again in front of people. It's more fun that way to find what works with an audience and what works with my personality too.

What do you like or dislike about comedy in New York?

I like the friends you end up making and seeing over time in New York. I have lifelong friends that I've been in the trenches with on jobs and on unpaid projects and we've really gotten to know each other through that. I also like finally meeting people in person after hearing about them for years on social media or in "the scene." I've met a few people who I've heard about for a long time and feel like I know them, and when I finally meet them it's nice to interact and realize we have a lot in common. I also live close to a lot of comedians in Brooklyn and I like running into them and hearing what they are up to. It's always cool to hear about other people's jobs and projects and be able to relate with others' experiences different than your own.

I dislike a lot of the fights on social media that comedians get so wrapped up in and then they're forgotten a week later. It feels like there is some witch hunt in media and comedy—like who should everyone hate or what show is the worst because of this thing, etc.—and people put so much energy into fighting about it online. I wish I could just mute all that and get to know other comedians in person and interact with them that way, not in a volatile comment thread. So I usually just stay out of it.

Who is the funniest person you know?

Wow, hard question. One would be one of my frequent collaborators Josh Lay (from Awful DJ). He has a hilarious and distinct way with words, phrases, people, personality, and body movements (he did theater all through college and was actually a professional NHL mascot for two years).

He is one of the few people I know that can coin specific sayings you will think are ridiculous and then two weeks later you find yourself using them all the time.

Another would be my mom.

Why are jokes funny?

Because they are surprising or smart or hit that thing inside you that says, "Oh yeah, I think that way, too."

They hit a place where you see something in a different way than you had before and you agree with what the joke is saying; you understand it. I heard a quote that says, "Friendship is born at that moment when one man says to another, 'You too? I thought that no one but myself...'" and I think the same thing is true with jokes. You see something and you agree with it and think *Me too! That's so true, I do that, I think that.*

It's the best with absurd things. I love seeing things that strike me as insane and fun and funny and I can't explain them. And I love finding out other people find those things funny, too. I just think, "Oh my gosh I love that so much too, that's insane."

Like skeletons? So funny. A skeleton making coffee? It's hilarious. Mostly you think of a skeleton being spooky or just dead, but think of it differently. For instance, tired in the morning and making coffee. LOL.

JENNIE SUTTON

🐦 *@unclejennie*

Jennie is a writer and stand-up comedian from New Jersey. She was a monologue writer for The Late Show with David Letterman. She is a writer/producer for Comedy Central's snapchat series "Goober Pool," and has appeared on The Wendy Williams Show, The She-Devil Festival, The Queen Bee Comedy Invitational, Albany Make Me Laugh and The Women in Comedy Festival. Her sketch team, Dollar Pizza, has been featured on Huffington Post, Funny or Die, MSN and the LA Times.

Where did you grow up?

I grew up in Montclair, New Jersey. It's a pretty typical suburban New Jersey town, temperate climate, wrap-around-porches, three Starbucks. There is that creepy old Victorian house down the road, with the old woman. Don't go there at night. She'll steal your youth.

What did your parents do for a living when you were a kid?

My mom was a dance teacher for most of her life now she's a guidance counselor. My dad was a drummer now he's a salesman for P.C. Richards.

Where did you first perform comedy?

In front of my parents while they were trying to watch TV. So, my living room.

What was the first bit you tried onstage?

"It's weird, I only see white people wearing those 'Life is Good' t-shirts."

How did you begin writing for The Late Show with David Letterman?

I worked there for about two years before writing for the monologue. I talked to the head writer about what I wanted to do. He saw I was doing stand-up and gave a haunted-town girl a chance. I still can't believe it. It was such an education to let go of my ego and write in someone else's voice especially David Letterman's. It was extremely humbling, incredibly rewarding.

What advice would you give someone who wants to write for a late night show?

There are lot of different ways to do it but a lot of people have been able to contribute to late night by stubbing their foot in the door. Get an internship, PA, do your job well and sometimes really nice people notice your hard work and tell them what you like to do!

What's your writing process like?

Whenever I can but I do like writing in the mornings and before I go to bed at night. Lately I've been writing on my roof. I also write in hotel lobbies, makes me feel like a sophisticated prostitute.

What do you like or dislike about comedy in New York?

I love how shitty it is! There's not really anything I dislike about it. I love New York and I love comedians. I get to watch them perform and hang out with them all the time which is pretty great.

Are female comedians disadvantaged?

Whenever I get my period I have to chill in my hut for like six days so I miss a lot of mics.

I don't think we're disadvantaged, per se. Many of the best comedians are women. It's about perceptions. People can be threatened by women in power and comedy is power. I've definitely felt 'otherized' at times. I've felt like a token at times. But the people who actually care about comedy know funny is funny.

What do you think about writing jokes on the internet?

The jokes that I don't think about or dwell on are the ones that get Retweets and Favorites. The jokes that I stew about don't get any attention. If I care about a joke personally it usually resonates with someone else. It's great to be able to connect with people in that way.

What are you working on now?

I'm doing as much stand-up as I can, trying to get better. I'm writing a lot of different things. I'm creating a web series. Doing fun things with my sketch group, Dollar Pizza. Aging. Very excited to age.

Who is the funniest person you know?

My dad.

Why are jokes funny?

Because they were fat in middle school.

ZACK BORNSTEIN

🐦 *@zackbornstein*

Zack is a Jimmy Kimmel Live Segment Director, writer at UCB Theater, host of "1000 Comics To See Before You Die" and creator of Garlic Jackson Comedy. He has directed, written, produced, and performed original comedy for ABC, Comedy Central, FOX, MTV, The New Yorker, and more. Birthed in Seattle, Zack studied Neuroscience at Brown U. and was selected as a Rhodes Scholar Finalist.

What did your parents do for a living when you were a kid?

My dad was a community psychiatrist, and my mom was a special education researcher. They are far better humans than I will ever be. Which I guess means they failed as parents, because I'm changing their legacy from helping people, to making dumb noises with my face-holes.

What was the first bit you tried onstage?

"Hi, my name is Zack, I like the name Zack, but I had to change the spelling to Z-A-C-K, because in elementary school when it was spelled Z-A-C-H, all the other kids would tease me by pronouncing it stanky fat ass bitch."

It's an easy misdirection, but it went over well and friends kept repeating it to me, so I opened every set in college with that joke but with a different punchline. By my senior year, people knew the joke, so that on my last show, I said the anti-joke,

"Zatch", and got a standing ovation from everyone there. It was the only time I've ever cried on stage; I was so happy. Felt like folks actually knew me for my dumb jokes.

Being a Rhodes Scholar Finalist at Brown isn't a typical entree to comedy. When/where did you figure out you could be a comedian?

My plan was to take a year off before medical school to apply for the Rhodes, and play around in comedy. By the end of the year, I was having fun doing comedy and had enough leads to make the jump.

I got first hooked at my Bar Mitzvah during the candle lighting ceremony (where you go through your family/friends and give them each a little shpiel)—I went off-book at one point and got a big laugh, and then did essentially crowdwork for the 200-odd guests. There was something intoxicating about that many people facing you and laughing together, and it's set me on this delusional hunt.

What's the secret to getting your foot in the door as a writer?

Write. It's free. After graduating I did a comedy shotgun-blast, trying everything and following anything that sticks—McSweeney's/New Yorker articles, Onion/Smew satirical news, stand up, sketch, UCB, reality TV, late night, etc. I must have had 100 different freelance jobs my first year out of school, and applied for 1000 more. In science they call that exploratory behavior, trying everything and then following the positive feedback, but I think it might just a marker of insanity.

Honestly, what ended up helping the most was 1) Making my own content—it's so easy and cheap these days! 2) Getting together with other folks who take comedy seriously, and 3) Making myself super easy to reach, people don't like clicking and typing to find your contact info.

What is Garlic Jackson? How did you guys get together?

My comedy production house & live troupe—we create sketches, web series, TV, online content, branded content, etc. We performed live shows and toured festivals/colleges, too. It began when my best comedy friends in college (Adam Wagner and Adam Weinrib) and I all moved to NYC and wanted to make sketches together, so we did.

We started with videos, then landed a live test show at The PIT through the great storyteller Kevin Allison. We handpicked the rest of the group from the most talented folks we knew in the comedy community. After our first show sold out, we got a second show, then we got a NYTimes blurb, and from there it was off to the races. Most of them still live in NYC, please help me convince them to move West. Seriously.

What's the hardest part about working in late night TV?

It's fast and relentless, so you don't have time to second-guess your own decisions, which I love to do. Is that a dumb thing to say? Oh jeez, it's too late to change it.

What do you like or dislike about comedy in Los Angeles?

I love meeting some of the most talented, hardworking, brilliant comedians working today. I don't love meeting the most hacky, mean, and pessimistic comedians on the scene today. You get both here.

Why do some jokes work on the internet and others don't?

Boy, do I wish I knew. I'd be a lot more successful. The internet is so chaotic, and beautiful, and impossible to predict. Every time I think something will do well, it tanks, and every time I think something will suck, it blows up. Or not. Who knows!

But it's nice to throw things at the wall, and essentially

quantify how funny a joke is. It's less nice that you never hear laughter, just numbers. It's not as viscerally satisfying.

Who is the funniest person you know?

My brother, Jake. Makes me laugh harder than any other human on the planet. I wish he wrote more comedy, but he's too talented for it, and writes serious things instead, seriously check him out: 🐦 *@jlbornstein*

Why are jokes funny?

That's my favorite question.

Also, what I was going to do my Rhodes study on (and correlated to brain activity). One of my best friends in college, Jamie Brew, and I used to discuss this all the time, because we were both comedy-science nerds. We have a lot of theories on it, but none that are that satisfying, yet. He has a great one about jokes being an exaggeration of known phenomenon. I have one about jokes being a way of connecting previously unrelated concepts. There's this professor in Maryland that showed how laughter is largely social. Like you don't laugh nearly as much when you're watching a show alone as when you're with friends. Or in a movie theater. Or in a conversation. But funny is weird. Is it just about surprise? No. Because not all surprises are funny.

I love this question, and if you have any thoughts, call me.

MICHAEL BRUMM

🐦 *@mbrumm*

Michael is a writer for The Late Show with Stephen Colbert and
previously wrote on The Colbert Report for nine years. He has won four
Emmy Awards and has written for Maxim and The New Yorker.

When did you realize that you could make a career in humor?

I still haven't quite realized that. I remember listening to a
radio interview with Harry Shearer and he said he only thought
he'd be in the business for a little while and then move on to
something more stable. Even though I've been doing this for 10+
years, I still kind of feel the same way. The panic of "this thing can
disappear at any moment" still looms over me.

> Some people are more confident with their career/lives.
> Those people are my heroes.

What is it about Chicago that makes for such funny comedians?

This may have changed over the years. But when I was doing
improv in Chicago, it seemed like people just did it because they
loved it. They weren't doing it to get famous; they were just doing
it to have fun. And there's something pure about that. There's
something about just doing something for the sake of it, without
trying to achieve anything, that frees you up to be funny.

What were the series of events that led you to writing for The Colbert Report?

It was mostly through improv and dumb luck. I knew this improviser named Ali Davis (great person), who worked for this company called Jellyvision, which makes the game You Don't Know Jack (great game). Anyway, she told me about a writing position opening at her company and I applied and got it. It was there where I worked with Allison Silverman (another great person), who would later go on to be the head writer and executive producer for The Colbert Report.

We stayed in touch over the years and, well, she was generous enough to give me a chance to apply for Colbert. So, to amend my opening a bit, I got my job mostly through improv, dumb luck, and the generosity of friends.

Are there any differences in writing for a cable network vs. writing for a nationally broadcast station? If so, how do they compare?

They're both kind of wonderful in their own way. While we were on cable, it felt like we were kids who were putting on a show. There weren't a lot of rules or adults around. We were just running around having fun. Broadcast is a little more adult, a little more corporate and buttoned-up. But you have access to bigger guests and bigger budgets, so you can do a bit more. So yeah, in my experience, they're a little different, but they're also both a lot of fun.

What advice would you give someone who wants to write for TV?

I would say embrace the crooked path. You don't have to go from college to LA to super stardom. Take the crooked path. Get a shitty job, go to grad school, get another shitty job that gives you insurance. Just keep trying along the way to get what you want. But if it doesn't happen right away, don't stress. Those shitty jobs and tangents along the way will give you material later on.

What's the hardest part about coming up with jokes every day?

It's getting used to the emotional roller coaster. You'll have good days and bad days. One day you'll pitch something that everybody loves. The next day you'll pitch something that really just unbelievably bombs. It's just getting used to that feeling. Knowing that when you're down, you'll go up, and when you're up, you'll go down.

But you get used to it. And, honestly, after a while, it is kind of fun to bomb, because those are usually the craziest, wildest pitches.

If you weren't a writer, what do you think you would be doing?

I've always fantasized about being a bike messenger. Whenever I see those guys get in the elevator, with their pants leg rolled up, their tattoos, and their shades, I always think, "Man, I wish I was that was me." So yeah, probably a bike messenger.

Or maybe just someone who creepily ogles bike messengers in elevators.

What makes a joke funny?

Fart sounds?

IMPROV

ARIANA LENARSKY

🐦 *@aardvarsk*

Ariana writes songs, stories, poems and jokes in Los Angeles. She does a podcast with Brittani Nichols and can be seen performing at UCB and The Virgil.

Lenarsky is a cool last name. Where does it come from?

Ellis Island. My grandfather Fievel Lenovsky came over on a submarine or whatever from Russia, and somebody at Ellis Island decided to change Lenovsky into "Lenarsky" to make it more Hollywood. He also changed a bunch of other Lenovskys into Leonards. So now I have a bunch of relatives running around with the last name Leonard that I'll never meet because it's so common a last name. And you know what? I don't give a fuck!

Did you grow up in LA?

I was born in Kentucky, to be honest. There was no real reason for it. My father worked at Kentucky Fried Chicken. We came to Los Angeles when I was four, and my parents swiftly divorced because they wanted me to go into comedy. My mother lived in Burbank and my father bounced around the city until he remarried and transformed into an Orthodox Jew. This was weird of him to do. Growing up in Burbank was weird too.

My brother and I rubbed shoulders with child actors, and we fielded several weird teachers who were unemployed actors and pretty bitter about it but still put on a good show for us kids. It was fun and weird and dumb. Jay Leno used to come glean the eight-year-olds for jokes during recess at my elementary school. On the weekends I was forced to go to keep shabbos and go to shul. What with the entertainment industry on the one hand and orthodox Judaism on the other, you really had to keep your eyes open. A lot of smoke and mirrors.

When did you realize you wanted to be a comedian?

I think being a comedian is something you're born with and then have to deal with for the rest of your life, like having cystic fibrosis or a super-hot mom.

How did you first get involved at UCB?

I think I sang my way onto the stage, which is cheating. I got cast in "Tonya Harding: The Musical!" as a chorus member.

How did that come together?

Jesse Esparza, a crazy kid with a big heart and a big mouth, had the idea about two years ago, and cobbled the more musically inclined comedians together to be in it. It was a pretty dark show. We showed a lot of the abuse Tonya received from her mother and her husband/accomplice Jeff Gillooly. Nancy gets clubbed in the show too, obviously (spoiler). We had to balance truly heinous, world-famous abuse with some pretty bright, silly songs.

But Jesse and his writing partner Manny Hagopian were fearless about it, and the women who played Tonya and Nancy (Leslie Korein and Heather Woodward) were disastrously, brutally talented. We sold out every performance for about a year and a half. I've never laughed harder during rehearsals. Also Tonya Harding is a tragic figure and should be awarded amnesty.

What are you working on now?

Dream City—a show I'm writing with my pal Lee Rubenstein about a struggling musician who thinks she's had the best idea in the world: to sing people to sleep for a living as a professional lullabyist. This is based on my real life, unfortunately. I'm also finishing up songs for a musical about Marie Curie, written by Sasha Feiler & Dan Black.

Any advice for someone who wants to get work published online?

Don't suck.

What do you enjoy most about writing jokes on Twitter?

I think I like knowing I made somebody else feel something for a second. I like trying to find a way to provoke and soothe a reader at the same time.

What do you like or dislike about comedy in LA?

I like the women and dislike everyone else.

Why are comedians good with words?

We have no other weapons.

What makes a joke funny?

If I knew, I wouldn't be a comedian.

ILANA GORDON

@IlanaAbby

Ilana is an iO Chicago Harold team performer. She originally hails from Connecticut, but currently lives in a state of continuous panic. You can read Ilana's written work on The Huffington Post, McSweeney's internet Tendency, Reductress, Mashable, The Second City Network, RedEye Chicago and on toilet stall doors across America.

When did you realize you wanted to be a comedian?

Growing up, I did a lot of musical theater, which I was fundamentally not good at. But I took this one acting class where we would do these improv exercises that I really enjoyed and felt really comfortable doing, so I thought there might be money in that. I was wrong.

What did your parents do for a living when you were a kid?

My dad was a computer programmer for an insurance company and my mom's career evolved as I got older. She's a cellist, so she did a lot of performance stuff when I was young, then she became a music teacher and now she's a school psychologist.

What kinds of tools did you pick up while studying screenwriting?

I came into college very green, so learning things like formatting and narrative structure were huge for me. But I think the biggest tool I picked up in college was discipline. I love to procrastinate and I'm also a huge perfectionist, so my first inclination is to put off writing something until I can write it perfectly. School taught me that it's more important to fart out a terrible first draft than it is to sit on a good idea forever.

What do you enjoy most about humorous fiction?

The great thing about writing for the internet is that now some of these platforms have such big audiences that you know people are going to see your work. And that's a nice perk — especially when you're used to working in live comedy.

In terms of the work itself, I love the challenge of taking something in the news and figuring out my take on it. Plus, I love how short the pieces are. I feel I do my best work between 350 and 472 words. Anything over 473 and it's all garbage.

How did you first get involved with iO Chicago?

I spent my last semester in college studying comedy at The Second City and I fell in love with Chicago. I ended up staying after my program ended and taking classes at iO. I got placed on a team in 2011 and I started coaching teams two years later.

Sweet! Which teams have you coached?

I've coached four Harold teams at iO (Attica, JTD, Blood! and Cecilia). It's one of my favorite things I get to do.

How does sketch-writing compare with writing for stand-up?

I like sketch writing because for a long time, I was scared to write or say the things I actually felt or believed. And with sketch, you can kind of filter your thoughts and ideas through the eyes of your characters, which makes it feel safer.

With stand-up, everything I say has to be rooted in something I actually feel or believe, otherwise I feel weird talking about it. So in some ways, I'm finding writing for stand up easier, because it's just me talking about the things that make me laugh.

Why do you think comedy works well in Chicago?

I think Chicago gives comics a lot of freedom to fail—there's not a huge industry presence here, so people are able to focus more on doing the work and taking cool risks than on building their personal brands. Also, there's an incredible sense of community here that I haven't seen anywhere else.

Why do you think comedians become comedians?

Because the world doesn't need any more happy, well-adjusted dental hygienists.

What makes a joke funny?

A smart, fast set-up and a punchline that takes you by surprise.

Also, ham-fisted references to Arby's (this portion of my thoughts brought to you by Arby's).

JULIE MARCHIANO

🐦 *@juliemarchiano*

Julie is a Chicago-based actor, writer, and improviser.
She is currently performing in The Second City e.t.c.'s 40th Revue, A Red
Line Runs Through It; and *Improv All Stars* at The Second City's UP
Comedy Club. As a writer, Julie has been featured on The Huffington
Post, The Second City Network, RedEye Chicago, The Paper Machete,
and in FRANK151, among others.

What is it about Chicago that produces so many talented comedians?

I think Chicago is a safe place to try and fail. It's a great city
to cut your teeth in, to see top-notch shows seven nights a week,
and to perform whatever you want almost anywhere you want,
whenever you want. I also think the weather honestly has a lot to
do with it. That probably sounds insane but follow me on this:
Chicago comedians are going out in blizzards to do an improv
show or a stand-up set like, nine months out of the year. We want
it really bad, and we have incredible work ethic, and those who
don't get weeded out.

What did your parents do for a living when you were a kid?

My dad has worked in transportation forever, and my mom
works in HR. They are very, very funny. My whole family is
very funny.

How did you first link up with Second City?

I came here for two weeks in the summer of 2010 for Second City's summer intensives. I watched the Mainstage show on my first night in town and thought, "Oh my God, this is my dream job." I think I said that out loud to a stranger, too. Anyway, I was a moron and moved to New York shortly thereafter. I lasted six months before I moved here, in February 2011. Around a year later, I got hired.

How does one become eligible for the Second City Touring Company?

Well, you have to have some training. I know what the rules are now but back in MY day, just to audition you had to have a year of improv training somewhere under your belt. But you know, you also have to be a good writer and a good actor. I think the auditions nowadays take a look at all of that stuff.

What kinds of things do you like about performing on the road?

I'm not touring anymore, actually. Touring was a hard job for me. I am a creature of habit and love being alone and there is no routine and no alone time on the road. But, the best thing for me, truly, was introducing people to The Second City. I mean, there is nothing better than having a kid come up to you completely blown away by what they just saw, asking every question they can about how they could do the same thing.

Ask anyone who works at Second City what made them come here, and half of them would tell you that they saw a Touring Company show when they were in high school or college and it changed their lives. We're CHANGING LIVES.

What are you working on now?

I'm really very lucky to have a full-time job in comedy, doing shows (at least) four nights a week at The Second City. Second City keeps me busy with other shows and projects, too (I'm writing this on a break from a workshop where I'm helping with the development of a new project with Second City's Theatricals division). Quite honestly, I've been working a ton lately to get out of credit card debt so I think I'll be more creative next month when that's all paid off. Just keepin' it real!

Why do you think comedians become comedians?

Man, I do not know. People assume that comedians are all disturbed, and I guess that's true to some degree. I always used to worry that because my life growing up was relatively normal and fun, I would never achieve the things I wanted to achieve, that jobs like mine would be reserved for people with like, a ton of unique life experiences.

I think I've always been weird and very observant, so I think there's something there — comedians are hyper-aware of the world around them and can't help but comment on it.

What makes a joke funny?

Well, I love seeing and reading jokes that are relatable, sort of along the same lines of what I said earlier?

Like when people call out something we all know or experience and put their spin on it. Specifics are huge for me. Like, it's so much funnier to say "Toyota Tercel" than "my car", right? Also, my jokes may not sound the same coming out of someone else's mouth, you know? If Amy Schumer started doing Brian Regan's jokes it would be f***ing weird, right?

So, I think good writing + developing your voice + being relatable in some way + some performance polish and/or rehearsed delivery = hopefully a badass joke.

CAITLIN KUNKEL

Caitlin is a comedy writer, director, and producer based in Brooklyn, NY. She teaches screenwriting and satire for The Second City and takes off her pants as soon as she gets home. She was a Fulbright scholar in Indonesia and has an MFA in Writing for the Screen and Stage for Northwestern. You are correct, she is NOT a millionaire with those life choices, thanks for noticing! Read more of her musings and check out her very professional avatar on Twitter.

Where did you grow up?

I grew up in the biggest little state in the union, Rhode Island. Specifically, Warwick, right by the airport.

Not the beach part.

What made you first want to pursue a career in comedy?

I came at comedy somewhat backward. I wrote VERY DRAMATIC THINGS for the entirety of my undergrad and graduate schooling and then the second I finished my VERY DRAMATIC graduate portfolio and sold a VERY DRAMATIC screenplay, the urge to write drama basically dissipated and was replaced with vast yearning to write comedy. I began taking classes at Second City Chicago and unfortunately fell deeply in love with sketch comedy, thus ensuring I would never make enough money in my lifetime.

What are some things you learned about writing while getting your MFA at Northwestern?

The most brilliant thing I learned was just how to structure something. A screenplay, a play, a short film, a TV episode. My MFA is literally in Writing for the Screen and Stage (another moneymaker!), so we went through a lot of different forms. Learning there were some rules to follow and that I wasn't out there alone, typing away, hoping it somehow came together, definitely helped free me from writer's block. Obviously once you know the rules you can break them, but just learning them in the first place helped console me that I wasn't always shooting entirely in the dark when I started writing a piece.

Also, I respond well to deadlines. Having to hit them 4–5 times a week makes you stop being a precious brat about your writing. Sitting in a workshop and hearing people seriously talk about something you wrote in three hours because you procrastinated so long you ran out of time made me stop procrastinating. I didn't want to feel like I was wasting their (and my) time. I think having a writer's group or someone holding you accountable for a volume of work is the best thing you can do for your writing.

Why is Chicago such a cool place to tell jokes?

Chicago is a true training ground. People love to learn and work hard to get better. I saw many less egos than I had expected. It's OK to go through a period where you only write sketches that are way too complicated or harsh and no one laughs at them on your way to a (slightly) higher hit rate.

How were you first introduced to the scene at Second City?

I had friends in graduate school who had taken classes and toured with Second City, and so I was curious about the vibe over there, even though I was terrified of performing. I got a grant to go through the entire sketch writing program — which takes just over a year. By the end, you've written an entire sketch review, produced it, cast it, and worked with a professional director. That experience is invaluable in terms of later going on to produce your own shows — just having already seen the entire process top to bottom lets you feel a lot more confident booking a venue and making a budget.

Why do you think it's been such an institution in the city?

Because it makes sense. Having taken classes there myself, having taught using the Second City methods, and written classes myself that are based upon it, I have seen hundreds (probably getting close to a thousand, at this point!) of people from different countries, different ages, different backgrounds, learn to mine their own experiences for comedy.

Second City tells people they have something important to say, then shows them how to get it out.

What's something that you often tell screenwriting students?

Stick with your idea and finish it. I teach an eight-week online class for Second called Story for TV & Film, and in the fourth week students choose one of the ideas they've brainstormed and gotten feedback on and begin to write a synopsis and outline for it. At week five pretty much everyone tries to change their idea, because they've become convinced that because they got stuck on plotting or character or details that week, they didn't choose the right idea.

The advice I give them is that pretty much every project will have moments like that, where you're puzzling out a solution and wondering if the pieces are going to eventually add up. Even if you end up not liking the final course product, you'll learn much more from sticking with a story and trying to make it work then having the start of three different projects.

So basically I say "don't give up" in a much more longwinded way.

What's the hardest part about writing?

Finding the balance between being critical and being creative. It's so hard to write and enjoy the process as you're seeing the things that aren't turning out the way you'd like. I try to write a nonjudgmental first draft before I let myself get in there and start cursing out my terrible writing and nonexistent sense of humor. Usually around the third or fourth draft I start to like the piece and myself again.

What makes a joke funny?

I always think that a kernel of truth, or the element of recognition, is what makes someone respond to a joke.

I've been to comedy shows where I came away convinced that comedians are the philosophers of our times, which is a very frightening thought in some ways.

RILEY SOLONER

@RileySoloner

Riley is an actor, writer, and comedy person originally from Albany, California. He has performed at the UCB Theatres in New York since 2009 as a regular in shows like *The Chris Gethard Show* and *Harold Night*. Riley is also known as Vacation Jason, who is best known for being on vacation forever. You can see Riley in web videos for IFC, UCBComedy, CollegeHumor, TheFlama, and Comedy Central.

What's interesting or uninteresting about Albany (California)?

The origin of Albany is quite interesting. It used to be called Ocean View and it was Berkeley's garbage dump. In 1908 a group of women grabbed some shotguns and rifles and scared off the garbage wagon drivers. From there, the people came together to turn Ocean View into its own city. A year later they voted to change its name to Albany.

It's a nice place. I remember it as a safe and friendly place to grow up.

What did your parents do for a living when you were a kid?

My mom stayed at home and raised me. Once I was old enough to walk myself home from school, she got a job as a secretary in a San Francisco law office. When she started, she barely knew how to use a computer. Instead of hiring anybody new when someone would leave or die, my mom's boss would just give my mom more and more responsibilities. She steadily grew into a total badass legal assistant that still finds the time to talk to me on the phone and watch my YouTube videos all day.

My dad can hustle. For many years, my dad worked at Interstellar Propeller. A company that manufactures and sells the "beany" baseball cap with the plastic propeller on top. As you can imagine, his work environment was a bustling factory not unlike Willy Wonka's Chocolate Factory or Pee Wee's Playhouse. It definitely wasn't a creaky house in Berkeley owned by a banjo playing hippy. My dad has done landscaping, he sold antiques at the Berkeley Flea Market, all kinds of odds and ends.

When he was my age, he was an expert at talking down people suffering from bad trips at Grateful Dead concerts in the medical tent. If anyone knows how that can translate into a career opportunity, please contact me.

What was the first bit or joke you performed on stage?

In middle school I started writing absurd, stream of consciousness poems. I read them on stage during the Tornado of Talent at Camp Winnarainbow, the performing arts summer camp led by hippy icon and ice cream flavor Wavy Gravy. They kind of became my calling card. I remember I had one poem about Godzilla. I wrote another about how much I disliked the trail mix snack I was given on a flight.

When and where did you fall into a groove as a performer?

I think the first time I fell into a groove that felt really influential and motivational was when I started making videos for YouTube when I was 18 or 19. In high school, I had a very eye opening video production class. I fell in love with the process of making these small scale, intimate projects. I got a used MacBook Pro as a graduation gift and started making shorts. I developed a very specific ritual for my process: Fold my futon into couch mode, pin a sheet to the wall behind me, set up my MacBook on a food tray on top of my laundry hamper, set up my desk lamp behind my MacBook on the cardboard box that Rock Band for Xbox came in, and improvise in character until I had something I was confident I could edit together. I would edit in costume so that I could pick up shots right then and there if I needed to.

That was probably the most consistently prolific I have ever been. I was very adamant about making and releasing one video per week. One time I had a week off from my job and so I made five videos. I'm still proud of them and that stretch of time because that was long before I worried about the millions of reasons I hold myself back from just throwing down and putting myself out there on a daily basis. Camera quality, lights, writing the perfect bit, whatever. I gained a small and cool following with those very simple videos. Sometimes I watch them and it makes me want to say forget it, I'm making something right now. They're good natured and raw, they're funny without overthought. You can see the joy through the low production value.

I currently feel "out of the groove" as someone who makes videos at the moment. With these old videos I made in 2007, 2008 there was some "fuck everything else, I have to make something" urgency. It's creeping up again inside my gut. I'm excited to see what I make next.

What went into creating Vacation Jason?

Vacation Jason started as a character I would do late at night for my friends when I was a counselor at Camp Winnarainbow. It's good natured and mostly clean comedy, but it's also antagonistic, like with every joke I'm saying: Look how much fun I'm having, you're going to hate yourself for laughing at this. Vacation Jason is a good example of a time I felt "out of a groove" as a performer and did something about it. I was deep into obsessing over my UCB improv classes, trying to be the best, aspiring to get on teams, the usual. When I moved to New York I had planned on steadily making and releasing videos like I had been, but I just hadn't done it. I wasn't in love with any idea except maybe just doing Vacation Jason. Instead of making a one-off character video like I had before, I made a bunch of extra short videos as my first "series," Vacation Jason's Island Flavors. They're all pretty low quality, even for me. But it definitely got a ball rolling in terms of putting out something that brought me joy, everything else be damned.

Meanwhile, I was an obsessive fan of The Chris Gethard Show back when it was a monthly stage show at the UCB Theatre. After a year of shows, Chris invited me to host the one-year anniversary show. It was at that show that Chris invited me to be a part of the Chris Gethard Show cross country adventure, which was a 12-day road trip from the UCB in New York to the UCB in LA. One of my only pitches for the trip was Vacation Jason and it was immediately rejected. Gethard told me Vacation Jason was so annoying that if I tried to do it on the trip, I may be sent home or knocked out. So that was my lightbulb moment: I wouldn't just be the fan of the show along for the ride, I would be the villain.

Long story short, I took a chance with this character I love playing and I eventually won over my comedy heroes with the dumbest bit ever. I did the bit in Austin, Texas and ended up performing a double encore for a very rowdy audience. I was even allowed to do the bit at the road trip's finale show at the UCB in LA.

It took me almost a year to follow through and write the stage version of Vacation Jason's Island Flavors. I had never written a show to submit to UCB before and it was my baby, so I wanted it to be perfect. I don't recommend trying to write your perfect dream sketch show right off the bat, because you will panic and give up more times than you will be able to count. But I worked out some bits at great shows like School Night and Gentrify and eventually put together a show I am still very proud of. It's basically my version of Pee Wee Herman's old stage show. I tried to do a good job of making it a fun and joyfully stupid variety show in 25 minutes.

Coconut Berry Lemon Tree was mixed really well! What was the inspiration behind the album?

One night after drinking with my improv team, I found myself alone in the Union Square subway station chanting 'Coconut, Berry, Lemon, Tree' to myself over and over. After a while I thought to myself, "Hey, that sounds like something Vacation Jason would say." So when it came time to make all of those Vacation Jason videos, one of the first ones I knew I had to write was a promo for his hip hop mixtape, Coconut Berry Lemon Tree. I made the video with absolutely no intention of ever making a real mixtape.

Years later I taught myself enough Garageband to figure out how to compose Island Girl, the song in the Vacation Jason UCB stage show. Then in December of the same year, I was invited to do a bit show called The Brooks Brothers Christmas Clambake at UCB. I was a huge fan of this show, so I really wanted to deliver. I spent the whole week writing and producing the song Christmas on the Beach. After I had those two songs in the bag, it didn't seem so impossible to actually make Coconut Berry Lemon Tree a reality. I plugged away at making some beats, wrote some lyrics, and asked my super talented friends Phil Augusta Jackson and Patrick Noth to write some guest verses in character. After we had everything written and produced, we recorded everything in one day. Patrick did an incredible job mastering the mix and making it sound nice. I'm really proud of Coconut Berry Lemon Tree. I like that it's funny for reasons beyond "Hey, I'm bad at rapping!" I don't think I'm an amazing rapper, but I like that the joke is that I'm this character, and that I actually made this thing. And surprisingly, it's not the worst thing ever! The mere existence of this mixtape was a total joke, and then it became a real thing. That is cool to me.

Who is the funniest person you know?

My seven and 10-year-old nieces are currently in first place. The older one recently got her first iPhone (how crazy is that?) and she is super into directing. It's very cool to watch them work together on their shows. I recently signed on to be their editor. I don't know how long I'll last. They are very specific and demanding.

What's on your horizon?

Lots of exciting stuff. I recently started my own religion, called Temple of the Milk Spirit. It has been an incredible journey thus far and I can't wait to see what the milk brings to my life next. I've been writing a lot of sketches that I want to turn into videos.

Be on the lookout for some more collaborations between me and the Human Fish himself, David Bluvband. I want them all to look and sound perfect, but I'm getting very tired of waiting for the stars to align so I might just grab my phone like my nieces and just get something done already.

What's the dumbest superhero name you can think of?

Wine. A superhero named Wine.

Why are jokes funny?

My friend Jordan, who is very good at bullshitting, told me this: laughter is an evolutionary trait.

It's the involuntary response your body makes when your mind discovers a connection between two things it wasn't aware of before that moment. So to laugh at a joke means you're delighted by the connection of bits of logic that are new to you. But like I said, Jordan is a really good bullshitter, and I never Googled any of this. So I can't be sure.

HALLIE HAAS

🐦 *@halliekhaas*

Hallie is a New York-based actor, improviser, and writer. She hails from the idyllic valley of Northampton, Massachusetts, "Where the coffee is strong and so are the women" (to be found on mugs everywhere); and obtained her B.A. in Theatre and Comparative Literature from Oberlin College. She performs sketch at the Upright Citizens Brigade Theatre NY with Maude team Monaco and wrote/performed original characters on the first two seasons of UCBTNY's Characters Welcome. She can be seen in the 2014 SXSW Grand Jury Prize-winning feature film Fort Tilden, and has performed theater throughout New York and regionally.

When did you realize you could be an actress?

I've been performing since I was seven years old, and I think I knew from the first time I stepped onstage as a newsie in Newsies that this was what I wanted to do with my life. Sell papes. But honestly, I was hooked from the start and essentially never stopped.

What was the first bit or joke you performed on stage?

Well, I hosted my middle school talent show, which I'm sure featured some exquisite bits, but I think the first written jokes I performed were part of a set I wrote while apprenticing at Williamstown Theatre Festival. Lewis Black taught a stand-up workshop and my bit was called "Hallie's Rack," about this wacky LiveJournal phenom that happened during high school. Oddly enough, one of the most popular lines was improvised and went something like "Richard felt like he had missed the boat, and Richard is the kind of guy who always liked to be on the boat." That was the summer I started seriously thinking about being a comedian.

What's the creative process behind *Characters Welcome* at the Upright Citizen's Brigade? How did the show start?

Characters Welcome ran as a workshop at UCBT for some time before it became an official house team. I was a member of the inaugural Characters Welcome team, which was a group of ten extremely talented writer/performers, almost all of whom had performed at the theatre previously. We'd start the month by pitching ideas and each week thereafter bring in a draft of our character, get notes from our directors and teammates, and then perform the piece at UCB East Village at the end of the process. It's an incredible gift to have this kind of structure and feedback for individual work. I learned so much on my two seasons with CW; in fact, almost all of the material for the one woman show I'm currently working on came from my time on the team.

What do you like or dislike about comedy in New York City?

The NY comedy scene is fantastic. I really appreciate how many different communities there are as well as opportunities to perform or see any type of show. Some comedians are doing real conceptual/experimental shit, and some are just writing knock-out sketches for Maude (UCBT House Sketch); both are great and both are what make NYC a killer place to see and make comedy.

What is Verbomania!? Name your three favorite verbs.

Verbomania! is a podcast about the coolest words you've never heard of! I'm big into vocab and language in general and I wanted to make something that was both erudite and funny. Each episode I invite on a guest and we discuss our words of the day and then play a host of ridiculous games I've invented. My favorite one is called "Make It German" (after the German tendency to make words by stringing a bunch of smaller words together). My guest and I trade off words until we have a whole new term and then we devise what it would mean. The game debuted and was especially successful in the Neil Casey episode.

Three favorite verbs! Do they have to be verbs? Three words I love right now are: sonorous, obfuscate, and plumb.

What do you enjoy most about teaching music, art and writing classes?

Children are brilliantly inventive and often very funny, but I think what I enjoy most is how present they are and therefore how present one has to be to teach them. Kids are there in the moment for every step, every song, every project - they are fully in the experience. So to be a good teacher, one also has to be fully in the experience and totally plugged in to what is happening - this can be exhausting, but is also deeply rewarding and can lead to beautiful spurts of creativity. Additionally, the lack of arts funding in many public schools is pretty tragic, so I think the kind of work that Story Pirates and after school art programs are doing is extremely important and I am committed to being a part of the effort.

How does performing on stage compare with performing on camera?

Oh wowza! This is a big one. It's very different. On stage everything is at least a little bit larger than life. You actually have to speak louder to be heard. There is a certain amount of theatricality that is necessary to a successful live show. "Presence," as they say, which, in my estimation, is just the ability to be on stage, know (but not flaunt) that you're on stage, and connect with an audience. Film is about condensing that intensity and presence. You speak at normal levels, sometimes even lower, and the performance is often seen through the eyes or the face, rather than the whole body.

This is of course not always the case and there are tons of amazing physical performers who strut their stuff on film, but I have found that I am most successful when my energy is very directed and precise, as opposed to on stage, where you need to be so receptive to your fellow actors and the audience that your energy needs to reach from your entire body through every audience member to the back wall of the theater. Can you tell I grew up doing plays? They're both incredible art forms, though, and it's fascinating to untangle what makes them work.

Who is the funniest person you know?

Probably Neil. Or this girl Hilary I used to live with. Once at dinner she said "I don't gamble except heavily on sports," and honestly how is that not a tweet already?! I'm trying to get her to do stand-up but she's Canadian and therefore humble and also she has a real job.

You're but thought ahead and brought a portable DVD player and three movies with you on the trip. Which movies did you bring?

The Court Jester, White Christmas & My Neighbor Totoro: Two 50s-era musicals starring Danny Kaye (a personal hero) and a Studio Ghibli feature about an imaginary fluff monster who can make trees grow.

Why are jokes funny?

A lot of what I think is funny comes from the choice and musicality of the language—timing, rhythm, emphasis.

But some people are joke wizards and work the math of the punch line, some can take a commonplace experience and blow it out to hilarity, and some jokes are funny just because they are. That's what's magical about comedy: if it makes you laugh it doesn't matter *why* it's funny! Who cares! You're laughing! And laughing is the best!

MATT FERNANDEZ

🐦 *@fattmernandez*

Matt's approach to comedy comes off as detached and nonchalant. Originally from Tampa, Matt has performed with some of the biggest names in comedy (Doug Benson, Aziz Ansari, Jim Jefferies, and Bill Burr to name a few). He has written articles for College Humor and Playboy. He's a Second City alum, and has been featured on Sirius XM Radio and Rooftopcomedy.com. Add to that performances at the Funny or Die Oddball Comedy Festival, SLO Comedy Festival, Crom Comedy Festival, Laugh Your Asheville Off, universities, clubs, and theaters throughout the country, as well as his disheveled appearance.

What's interesting or uninteresting about Tampa?

Interesting: It's the lightning capital of the United States. Uninteresting: Mitchell. He's just this dumb guy I know. Not interesting at all.

Why did you first want to start performing comedy? What was the first joke or bit you tried on stage?

I thought I might be good at it, and I didn't want to work in a cubicle. My life had zero direction up until that point. I don't remember a specific bit. It was all the hacky stuff most comedians start off writing about; strip clubs, midgets, strip clubs that only employ midgets.

What advice would you give a comic trying his/her work published?

Write your ass off. There are websites who will publish your work, but don't pay anything. I started there and wrote about literally anything I could think of. I think it's easier to write about something you really love or really hate. Then after a year or two of that, I started submitting to better websites, and eventually got published.

Second City has churned out some of the world's most talented comedians. What is it about that place that allows talent to flourish?

A great staff who genuinely cares about what they're doing. I had a great teacher while I was there. Plus, I think the history helps a lot. It's like going from high school to collegiate sports. If you're good at basketball, you go to Kentucky or North Carolina to get great. If you're good at football, you go to Ohio State or Alabama to get to the next level. If you're funny, and want to learn how to use it and what to do with it, you go to Second City.

Do you prefer forming jokes on paper or on stage? Why?

Paper. Writing is my favorite part of it. That's actually what I went to Second City for. I always have a notebook and pen around, or I'll write notes in my phone sometimes. Getting into the habit of writing down anything you say or think of that you can use on stage is necessary.

How are comedy festivals unique, compared to clubs or theatres?

Comedy festivals are like comedian summer camp most of the time. In clubs and theaters, you go, you do your show(s), and you go home. At festivals you do your shows, then you hang out because there are 10–20 other comics around to hang out with and meet. I guess it'd be like going to work on a normal day vs. going to a week-long seminar where you meet all the people who work at all the different branches of the company where you work.

What do you like or dislike about the comedy scene in Tampa?

Tampa is the perfect place to start stand up. The scene is just big enough where you can get plenty of stage time and there are tons of clubs and rooms all over Florida. The only thing I dislike about the scene here is that the audience is all people who live in Florida. So you'll occasionally get the middle-aged woman downing Mich Ultra and being obnoxious.

Or the guy who shows up in a denim vest like that's a thing you can just wear. But for the most part, Tampa and St. Petersburg (just outside of Tampa) have a great appreciation for the arts despite what Lena Dunham would have you believe.

Who is the funniest person you know?

I don't want anyone who reads this to get their feelings hurt, so I'll just say it's irrelevant because none of them are funnier than me.

Why are jokes funny?

Because the person writing and telling them is funny.

Your dad telling a corny joke is never going to be funny because your dad isn't funny, and the person who came up with the joke originally probably wasn't that funny. Just like anything else a joke is only as good as the person who makes it.

MICHAEL WOLF

@mjwooolf

Michael is a comedian, writer, actor and filmmaker living New York City. He currently writes, directs and produces the longstanding MTV Series After Hours and is a regular performer at the Upright Citizens Brigade Theater

Where did you grow up?

I grew up in Massachusetts. My town was a very small rural town and I grew up on a somewhat defunct farm, although we had a variety of animals at different times. I spent a lot of time in the woods as a kid. I loved the forest and there were trees and rocks to climb and all that good stuff. My neighbors had peacocks and people don't know this, but peacocks scream. A lot. And it sounds like a person dying. I use to hate cities growing up because they made me nervous.

Where did you first perform comedy?

I went to a "Doctor Camp" (National Youth Leadership Forum on Medicine) when I was in middle school and I slowly realized I didn't want to be a doctor at all. Took another 10 years for the [feeling] to settle in. But the thing that excited me the most was the talent show at the end of the week.

I wrote a song about a sad clown and I made the kids in my group do interpretive dancing behind me. It was so stupid but I loved it. I guess that was the first time I performed. I used to make videos in high school too. Then I started doing improv in college and occasionally stand-up.

What was the first joke or bit that you tried onstage?

"I get congested a lot but pharmacies have started regulating how much Sudafed you can buy because make meth out of it. So I've started buying meth and making Sudafed. I'm just that congested."

Can you talk about The Triplets of Kings County? How did you guys assemble? What's fun about it?

It was my first big project in N.Y. Colin and Terence are actual brothers. Colin and I went to the same college but didn't meet until after. The three of us had similar sensibilities and would hang out and talk about what we wanted to make.

We loved Stella and Mighty Boosh. A web series felt a little stale to us so we wanted to do something very narrative driven that followed story structure but also something very silly. As our Anthony Apruzzese put it: "You guys lean into the stupid."

We started writing because Terence had a great back yard with a cool blue wall and I thought it would look nice to shoot on. So we called it Patio Boys and it was going to happen on the patio. First episode would be about throwing a housewarming party. But we wanted our characters to fail. The house wasn't properly warmed because they weren't popular enough and got cursed with a ghost. That made us laugh a lot so we decided to focus on the supernatural but only treat it like the everyday mundane.

I shoot, edit and direct a lot. I've learned to only take on projects I actually care about. And that every step is an opportunity for storytelling. Never go with the obvious choice. Push yourself to think of how you can match content and form and how to subvert expectations.

What projects are you working on? What do you do at MTV?

My biggest projects are NANCY (NancyComedy.com) which is my two-person musical comedy duo. We have an album and a show at UCB. Also OSFUG (osfug.com) which is my sketch group and we got some big stuff coming. At MTV I show run the video series After Hours with Josh Horowitz. I write, produce and direct sketches and interviews.

What do you like about the New York comedy scene?

I like how talented and hardworking it is. People are constantly making new and amazing things. I feel like it can be very supportive, a lot of people collaborating and building great shows together. I don't like how success oriented it feels.

Might just be where I am, but there's a sense of validation needed through commercial approval and getting recognition online. That's fickle.

Why are jokes funny?

Because they remind us that life is absurd and we're all floating in nothing. They are anarchic and it's exciting.

CHEYENNE GROGAN

🐦 *@cheyennegrogan*

Cheyenne is an actress, improviser, stand-up comedian and writer currently residing in Los Angeles. In addition to being the host for Gurl.com, she's booked national commercials for Converse, Purina, Kohl's, and many more. She studies improv and sketch comedy at Groundlings and the Upright Citizen's Brigade. She is a Screenwriting major in the Cinema and Television Department at California State University, Northridge. Cheyenne is the most beautiful person in the entire universe and totally didn't write this bio herself.

Where did you grow up?

I was born and raised in California in the boring town of Agoura Hills. People call it "The Bubble" because it's so tiny and everyone feels trapped. I should run their tourism department.

What's interesting or uninteresting about Agoura Hills?

Hm, I think this is pretty interesting: It is almost statistically impossible to go anywhere outside your house without seeing someone you know or at least recognize.

It's actually pretty terrible. You want Flamin' Hot Cheetos at 3am from 7–11? Boom, there's Jenny from your high school just dying to know "What's new with you??!?!"

What do your parents do for a living?

My mom is a chiropractor and my dad is a college professor. So, I'm super connected in the industry.

What was the first bit or joke you performed on stage?

The first bit I performed on stage was when I was 18. I talked about how "I smoke pot because I have glaucoma...and I like to get high." Then went into this bit about how when I'm high I like to do normal stoner things like eating way too much, watching TV, and reenacting the Torah. It was odd doing this at The Comedy Store and then having to be escorted out immediately after because I wasn't 21.

What do you enjoy most about improv? What do you enjoy most about stand up? How do they compare?

With improv, you can literally 'make stew out of anything.' Susan Messing said that from the Annoyance Theater in Chicago and it's *so* true. There are no mistakes because we can just get up there, play like kids, and keep discovering things about ourselves, our relationships, our surroundings, etc. It doesn't stop!

With stand-up, I enjoy the writing aspect (obviously). It's almost like a science because you have to dissect each joke to get to the funny. You might have a five-minute funny bit, but really, it can be trimmed down to a one minute, solid genius bit. I think being present in both stand-up and improv is what makes a successful comedian. In improv, if someone makes a mistake or does something weird, you call it out and make it part of your scene. It's similar in stand-up and with doing crowd work. We call out the odd things in life and put it in our sets. Following the unusual is what we do in comedy!

Sorry, this is douchey-ly long.

Are you working on any screenplays now? If so, can you share the premise to one or two?

Yes! I am! I have to ask Judd Apatow if that's ok first...Who am I kidding? We're BFFZ of course it's ok.

I'm working on an adaptation of the book "I'm With The Band" by Pamela Des Barres. It's about a biography about her life in the 60s as a groupie/girlfriend to many rockstars like Jimmy Page, Chris Hillman of The Byrds, and many more. It'd be fun to share her POV— I think it'd make a good unconventional comedy.

GURL.com seems to have a really fresh, tailored voice. How did you start hosting there? What's the creation process?

Yes! Gurl is amazing and is just super inclusive source for all females. I auditioned last winter and booked it by adding in my own jokes and stuff in the room. I get an already hilarious script written about certain health topics and just add in jokes/change jokes to make it more "my style." Who would have thought I would have my own style when it comes to talking about IUDs and periods? ...But, I guess I do.

Do you prefer forming jokes on paper or on stage?

Definitely on paper. I would love to be like Louis C.K. Or the late Patrice O'Neal and be able to go on and off paper, but I'm gonna need to be doing stand-up for 15 more years, live in my sister's house, and be way more bitter to be able to do that.

What do you like or dislike about comedy in Los Angeles?

I really enjoy how welcoming everyone is. You're gonna have douchebags in any field, but most people I've met are just eager to perform and have fun on stage, which is great. It really is a community and I love that so much.

Who is the funniest person you know?

My mom. I got my sense of humor from her, for sure. When I was little, she would pack me a "decoy lunch" and give me a paper bag with a potato, an onion, a stray household object, and a note that'd say something to the extent of: "You're as special as your lunch!"

What makes a joke funny?

Because both the unexpected and the truth are funny.

Whether someone says something unexpected or truthful, the audience finds a way to relate it back to themselves.

If something shocking (unexpected) is said, one reason someone may be laughing is because they can't imagine themselves sharing that absurd point-of-view. Or, if a truthful observation is said, the audience may laugh because they've had that same thought, too. I've had a lot of time to think about this…right before I start reenacting the Torah.

ANIMATED SHOWS

MARY HOULIHAN

@maryhoulie

Mary is a stand-up comedian, writer, actress, animator, and visual artist living in Brooklyn, N.Y. She has appeared on Jimmy Kimmel Live! and Billy On The Street, and has created animated shorts for Comedy Central.

Where did you grow up?

I grew up in Allendale, New Jersey, which is about 25 miles from Midtown, Manhattan if you are driving; but less miles if you are just drawing a straight line on a map.

What did your parents do for a living when you were a kid?

My dad was a banker and my mom worked in a yarn store, and is an avid knitter who travels to yarn expos and state fairs to participate in knitting contests and seminars. She has won several blue ribbons for her knitwear.

When & where did you first perform comedy?

I began doing comedy when it dawned on me that I could work towards being a television writer and performer by doing comedy. Previously I thought you had to go to Harvard and write for the Lampoon, or go to some other Ivy League school and major in writing for TV and Film, and get an internship at The Daily Show when you're 19; so I thought TV writing was out of the question since I didn't do those things. As soon as I learned different, I started taking improv and sketch classes at UCB, and then after a year of that I worked up the nerve to try stand-up. So my first improv performance was at UCB East, and my first open mic was at Eastville Comedy Club.

What was the first joke or bit that you tried onstage?

My first jokes were all about breaking up with an ex-boyfriend and moving to New York to do comedy. I thought it was a hard rule that you should be confessional in your comedy, but later became more interested in absurd situations and characters, instead of talking about myself so explicitly. I think the jokes about breaking up with the ex were funny and good, but eventually it felt like, we've been broken up for a year now, why I am still talking about this?

How did you start about painting stuff for people?

I went to college for painting. When I moved back to my parents' house and started doing comedy, I would spend my time at home working on these big paintings and drawings, and thought I would try to figure out how to get my work shown, since New York is the art capital of the world and all.

But I didn't want to schmooze at gallery openings, and I didn't want to do free labor for a gallery in Chelsea, which seemed to me to be the pathways to getting people to look at your stuff. I moved to Brooklyn and slowly stopped painting and just focused on comedy at night and dog walking in the day. Then after a while felt like I should get back in the habit, so I painted a couple dogs that I walked, and posted them online. Facebook friends wanted to buy them, so then I kept painting more portraits, and taking commissions to paint people's pets or friends or favorite celebrity or whatever, until that became the main source of my income. The paintings I make now are smaller and simpler than the things I used to make when I wanted to be a gallery artist, but I'm selling a ton of things and getting them seen by lots of people, and doing it on my own and not having to schmooze, so it is kind of funny how that stuff works out.

How did Cartoon Monsoon originate?

Cartoon Monsoon is an episodic live show about Mary, Joe, and Puppet, three friends and roommates who go on adventures, get visited by weirdos, and watch cartoons. The characters are played by myself, Joe Rumrill, and puppeteer Tim Platt. We wanted to have a show that featured animation and live comedy, so we made a show that is kinda similar in format to Peewee's Playhouse, where cartoons play between live bits. We just finished a weekly run at the Annoyance Theatre in NY. We basically felt like we had to write a new episode every week just to get our friends to keep coming back and paying the eight dollars to get in, and that if we did the same exact show every week people wouldn't want to come back. So that desperation to keep it new and exciting and different every week forced us to write a new script, make new props, and just learn a whole new show every week, which was really crazy and energizing and fun. Felt like we were making The Muppet Show or something.

What do you like or dislike about comedy in New York?

I love that there's room for everything. I love that you feel like always creating and making something new. Friendly competition based on mutual admiration. I don't like bitterness. I don't like petty stuff, negativity. Sometimes I wish everyone would just take a step back and realize we're all doing the same thing, even if we're going about it a different way. One person's success is everyone's success.

Why do some jokes work on the internet others don't?

I like simple jokes. One-liners. Misdirections. Twitter's great for those things. I love pretending to not get stuff, pretending to not understand how social media works. Taking things too literally.

I think a lot of that comes from the jokes I liked as a kid (and still like)—stuff like Deep Thoughts by Jack Handey, Zucker Brothers films, Steve Martin, Mel Brooks, Woody Allen. So much of that stuff depends on people coming off as buffoons because they take things too literally. "Don't call me Shirley" kinda stuff.

But those things only work if the audience/reader knows it's on purpose, and you don't always get to perform live for people who have all the same references as you, so that can make for a really tough environment for those kinds of jokes.

Who is the funniest person you know?

My best friend Sam Taggart makes me laugh a lot.

Why are jokes funny?

Sheesh I don't know.

I guess laughter is a response to being intellectually surprised, and it feels great so you keep trying to experience it and elicit it from others. I guess it's pretty boring to talk about, really. It makes life a lot easier when you laugh, so there is a biological imperative.

Oh man, I'm really boring myself.

JULIA PRESCOTT

🐦 *@juliaprescott*

Julia is a writer and stand-up comedian from North Hollywood. She's written for Cartoon Network, Nickelodeon, Disney, Nerdist, VICE, Geek & Sundry, and more. Her Simpsons-themed podcast, "Everything's Coming Up Podcast" is frequently featured in the Top Comedy Podcasts on iTunes. Her debut comedy album, "Every Joke on This Album Kills (because I cut out the ones that didn't)" will release in 2017.

What's interesting or uninteresting about North Hollywood?

A lot of people hear "North Hollywood" and think, 'Oooh ahhh… Hollywood sign, Walk of Fame, etc.' It's like a weird trick that we play on outsiders since it's actually a good 15–20 min. drive from all of that. It feels kind of sneaky, and in my opinion reflects accurately on the tone North Hollywood exudes as a place. We're like, one degree off always. We have an Arts District!
… kind of.

We have tons of theater! …with pun-heavy names. It's kind of where people go when they first get off the bus into town, so there's a lot of "gotta sing gotta dance / Up with people" kind of actors floating around. It is much different now than when I was growing up, though. They have a LAEMMLE now—Jesus, 17-year-old Julia needed a local art house theater like Bono needs a beer. North Hollywood is kind of the less cool younger sibling to Hollywood proper. Also the NohoArtsDistrict Twitter account is the funniest non-comedy twitter I follow.

What did your parents do for a living when you were a kid?

Here's the extremely Hollywood part about my upbringing—they came to LA to make it. I'm first generation LA, baby! My dad was a comedian and my mom was pursuing acting. I think they met doing community theater, so everything checks out. My parents divorced when I was four, and since then kind of found their own paths pursuing different careers. They're really inspirational to me and are the living embodiment of finding ways to keep that creative momentum going no matter what. That lesson alone has been a guiding force in my own creative pursuits—that it's not as *make or break* as people chock it up to be. You're not defined by a casting director or a show runner telling you yes or no. You have agency over your own creativity and you make the rules.

Growing up, my mom was appointed the head of the theater program at our church, and she always did really cool, creative things. I remember a great production of War of the Worlds she put on at the church. That's right. Next to Jesus on the cross was a cardboard set piece of some Martian shit. She was always thinking outside of the box and was a pretty cool Christian in that way. She knew it didn't have to be Jesus walkin' and talkin' 24/7. Besides, we already know Jesus chilled hard—what else you got?

What was the first bit or joke you performed on stage?

Oh boy. It was a joke I really, really loved and one I did for years after. Perhaps too long. But that's how it always feels. I came out onstage and pretended I was overly nervous—I mean "pretend" is really not applicable here. I was nervous as hell. I go out and say, "Man—I'm so nervous I forgot my first joke!" and people maybe react like, "Aww." And then I say, "But I was just talking to my friend Tyrone the other day and he said if that happened I could just borrow one of his jokes—so here goes." And then I pause and pretend to "get into character."

I milk the silence and then just shout, "Y'ALL LIKE TITTIES???" I go on from there, but that's the gist of it. It was a great way to combat that nervousness, and I can accurately say that I've shouted "titties" at the top of my lungs, to several different kinds of audiences from different backgrounds, age brackets, and so on—in front of my parents, in front of my friends. Everyone has now heard me shout "titties."

Friday Night Film School is a really neat thing. What was the original inspiration for the series?

I've always been a huge cult movie nerd. I used to run a cult film club called, "Film Corps" in high school and college. I would play a movie and make snacks around the theme of it. For "Cannibal the Musical" I made chocolate pudding "dirt" with body parts and gummy worms, stuff like that. I always wanted to make a nerdy cook book or something like that, but never had the time or the outlet to do it in.

Then one night I was driving around with my friend / hilarious comedian Dave Child and we were going to karaoke together, something we fully observe as ritual. I mentioned always wanting to do something with it and he said, "How about a podcast? We could co-host it and if you wanna make treats…I'll eat them." We quickly found out eating on the air wasn't great for listeners, but we continued on with the podcast. We had a ton of fun with it—a definite highlight was doing our first live show in the basement of Lost Weekend Video in San Francisco to a sold-out crowd. That was insane.

Can you talk about how Everything's Coming Up Podcast started?

My pleasure. When Allie and I first met, we were introduced by fellow comedian Will Weldon at a birthday party. He grumbled something like, "Oh hey, you guys both like the Simpsons. You'll get along." and then left us to it. I told Allie I was about to get a tattoo of the gummy Venus de milo and she told me she wrote a song about Milhouse, a friendship love story had sparked. Though

I was co-hosting a Simpsons trivia night at Meltdown comics once a month, I talked to Allie about wanting some kind of outlet to discuss the philosophy of the Simpsons at length. Or just quote it a bunch with fellow nerds. We talked about doing a podcast together and then spent the next month or so trying to figure out what that would look like.

I remember sitting with her at Little Joy during a comedy show and having our friend Brent Weinbach shout out fake name suggestions for it to distract us. "The Simpsons Chicks!" "Full House!" something like that. We settled on, "Everything's Coming Up Podcast" because it was so upbeat and was a subtle enough reference to the show while still explaining to strangers what our dang podcast was all about.

Our first guest was Alex Hirsch, who couldn't have been a better choice. Alex is the brilliant mind behind Disney XD's "Gravity Falls" a show that he describes as a mutant baby of "Twin Peaks" and the Hellfish episode of "The Simpsons."

Allie and I are similar kinds of go-getters. I often describe us as, "Type A and Type A-minus." We know when to lead and when to take cues from the other if they wanna take the wheel. One thing that we hear all the time, much to our delight is that our show stands out because it's apparent that we're good friends. "We like each other!" as Allie would always say. Even though that sounds like a "duh" part of the ingredients list for a podcast, it's pretty hard to master in my experience. Going forward, Allie and I have huge plans for the future. We wanna go on the road and do stand-up/variety shows with the podcast. We wanna transition more into on-camera stuff. We wanna interview every possible Simpsons creative person we can get our hands on. It's by far, one of the best things I currently get to do.

Do you prefer forming jokes on paper or onstage?

I like a little bit of both. It's hard for me to write out a joke entirely—I'll scribble down random premises, or maybe tweet something and revisit it later but my favorite parts of my jokes happen in the moment on stage. My boyfriend Mike has been tremendous in helping me get my head together post-show, because I used to just be in that post-show black-out where I don't quite remember what I said. He's great about talking with me about it after—and I've grown really accustom to it. Not only do I trust his opinion, but I always know what he's saying is coming from the best intentions. We joke that it's like we're "working on the family business" when we talk about it. He's a brilliant animator that works in comedy animation, so he knows his shit—he's not just talking out of his ass or saying nice things just to say them. He gets it.

Who is the funniest person you know?

Joe Wagner. Hire him, world. He will brighten any writer's room—guaranteed.

Why are jokes funny?

Because they're a break from monotony.

They're unexpected. They have the ability to be both silly and poignant.

JAK KNIGHT

🐦 *@ItsJakKnight*

Originally from Seattle, Jak is an LA-based stand-up, writer, and performer. He has been featured performing on Comedy Central's The Meltdown with Jonah and Kumail, @midnight, and the upcoming third season of Adam Devine's House Party. He has also written for Lucas Brothers Moving Co. on FXX. Jak performed at the main stage of 2015's Oddball Comedy Festival headlined by Amy Schumer and Aziz Ansari, and on the road has opened for various stand-ups including Joel McHale, Eric Andre, Moshe Kasher, and Dave Chappelle.

Can you walk me through the day you decided to move to LA?

Moving to L.A. wasn't out of some foreseen life-long goal. I did stand up once my senior year of high school because my homegirl Maria & Darius made me. Ate a cold dick! Graduated and listened to all my friends get scholarships and jobs and ideas of what they wanted to do with their lives. So, out of fear, I told everyone I'm moving to L.A. next month…. and did.

How do you decide what you want to talk about on stage?

I'm not good at jokey-jokes. Whatever I'm talking about is usually just bits and pieces of faded (under the influence) rants I've had with friends. From depression to pussy jokes.

What was on your shirt during your Meltdown set?

Hahahaha! It was a Scottie Pippen shirt my manager got me.

Why was it blurred out?

Couldn't get it cleared and I'm an idiot.

Lucas Bros. Moving Co. is very funny and unique. What led to you joining as a writer on the show?

The Bros are fuckin' hilarious. We met around the comedy community. They brought me in for a meeting to just talk really. We riffed the premises of about three episodes right then and there. Nick Weidenfeld, the show runner, was like "Yeah, you're hired" that day. Hear that kids!! Packets are pointless!

What makes for a good writer's room?

Playing your position. Say a writing room is the Golden State Warriors. I'm the Leandro Barbosa. I just come in and say funny shit and shut up. Let the Harvard guys be Harvard guys, let the show runner show run, let the quiet weirdo genius who randomly drops the line to fix everything do him. The writers room is a team! Respect everyone and from my experience you'll get a good product.

What have you learned about doing comedy on the road?

The road is my favorite… that's a young comic thing to say but when I'm in L.A. I don't get as much stage time as I want. The road usually gives me a lot of stage time and I'm in a city I've never been in, meeting new people. It helps build perspective for comedy and I love strip clubs. Comics who don't like the road are lame! Congrats, you can make people exactly like you laugh in Silver Lake woohooooooo.

Is Drake the best rapper in the game? Why or why not?

Kendrick Lamar is the best rapper. Drake is the best popstar. Drake has made the same album over and over throwing out weaker and weaker bars. ALL THIS BEING SAID... CONTROLLLLLAAAAAAAAAAAA. Love that shit! TURN THE 6 UPSIDE DOWN ITS A 9 NOW.

Why do you think comedians become comedians?

From what I've seen—a mix of traumatic experiences and over confidences. It's the most pompous thing to do. Hey! Everyone listen to me just talk!

What makes a joke funny?

People laughing at it. Plain and simple.

MIKE BENNER

@benner

Mike is a television writer. He has written for *Bob's Burgers*, *Gravity Falls*, the new *Danger Mouse* reboot, and other stuff you've never heard of. He also produces and co-hosts a monthly live comedy show called MIXTAPE. He also writes recaps of *Mystery Diners* for Previously.TV, for some reason. He's also on Twitter. He lives in Los Angeles. He is originally from Philadelphia. He's okay.

How did you lock down the 'benner' handle on Twitter? Was there stiff competition for that?

I just waited out the dude that had the handle. Twitter used to suspend users who weren't active for a while, and I knew that @benner didn't tweet much. And I wanted that handle. So I would just check his page regularly, and the moment I saw his account was deactivated, I pounced and changed my username from @michaelgbenner to @benner. It was the closest I'll ever come to big game hunting, and it felt amazing.

When did you realize you wanted to be a writer?

Writing is just a thing I kind of always did. I wrote stories and comics for fun as a kid. I was also obsessed with TV. I watched everything. I was basically raised by TV. So when I got to the age where I could wrap my brain around the fact that a group of humans were writing the things I was watching, it just sorta coalesced for in my brain. "Oh, TV writer. I wanna do that!"

What did you parents do for a living when you were a kid?

My parents worked various retail jobs over the years. Still do.

How did you start writing for Bob's Burgers?

I was hired as an executive assistant to the showrunners, but I knew I wanted to be on the writing staff. So, I developed a risky strategy: be terrible at my job.

A good assistant is always available to answer phones, run errands, do administrative work, etc. That was not me. I was constantly in the writer's room pitching. I missed calls, I dropped the ball, I was constantly playing catch up with my assistant duties. But I kept getting pitches into the show, so they wound up giving me a freelance script, and then after that I was hired on as a staff writer.

It worked for me, but I'm not sure it's a strategy I would recommend everyone try.

I saw you also worked on King of the Hill. Is there something that you especially enjoy about working in animation?

I never intended to get into animation, but it just kind of kept working out that way for me. And that's fine because I love it! I think the best aspect to writing for animation is that, when you're doing animation for a network, you get a lot of swings at an episode before it ends up airing. You get to crack an episode open and work on it at least three or four times between the script read and when it finally airs a year later, so you really can fine tune a moment or a joke a story beat until you're sure it works. It's nice.

But it does take a long time to see your work show up on a TV screen, which I will admit is frustrating. I can be impatient when it comes to work.

What inspired Mixtape LA? It seems to be the only show in town that unites rap and comedy.

I love stand-up with all my heart, but I was getting kind of sick of driving all over LA and standing in long lines to see shows, a lot of which would feature mostly straight white dudes talking about the same stuff. Then one day I kind of realized, "Hey, I can just put together the show I wanna see with the comics I wanna laugh at." So, with no experience producing a show, I just launched the show I wanted to see, and I've just been figuring out how to produce a good comedy show along the way.

I started out hosting it with my friend Peter Moses, a very funny writer and actor. We had no idea what we were doing, but we just kind of felt it as we went. We booked this dude Garrick Bernard on the show a few times and I thought, "This guy is one of the best young standups I've seen in a while." We got to know each other and he just reminded me of myself, but younger and funnier, so I replaced myself with him as co-host. So now he and Peter host it, and I produce it. Along the way, we just kind of figured out how to make a great comedy show.

As for what inspired the actual format of the show, I grew up on DJ Clue and Funkmaster Flex mix tapes in the '90s, and I'm just trying to put together the comedy show equivalent. We cram as many comics in as we can with a constant focus on building a diverse lineup. We show sketches. We leave a soundboard on stage so comics can blast reggae airhorns or drop Flex bombs if they want, which is one of my favorite touches of the show. We blast hip hop in between sets, and I honestly slave over the playlist each week. And once in a while we actually get a real rapper to come do a set, which is always the biggest thrill for me when that happens.

I don't know why, but modeling MIXTAPE after actual mix tapes... it's just my ideal show format.

Why don't those two genres don't overlap more often?

I think I'm about the millionth person to make this observation, but rap and comedy have a ton of overlap! Good rappers are usually funny and treat two or four bars like a joke: setup, punchline, setup, punchline.

I mean, there are so many rappers with a good sense of humor. Biggie was funny! Kanye is funny! Cam'ron is funny! Even Kendrick Lamar — by far our most self-serious rapper--has equated Martin Luther King, Jr.'s "Dream" to his own personal dream of having an Eiffel Tower-sized dick so he can have sex with the planet Earth. That's some very funny shit.

And obviously, a handful of rappers have invaded the comedy world. Snoop Dogg just did a season arc on Canadian sitcom Trailer Park Boys. Ice Cube stars in like one out of every five studio comedies these days. A$AP Rocky and Nas had some of the funniest lines in that "Popstar" movie. I don't think The Lonely Island will rest until they have collaborated with every living rapper in the world.

Some have already set up shop, but I think there's plenty more room for rappers in the comedy world. Every sitcom should have a rapper on it. Redman should play the wacky neighbor on every show ever. I'm only like 5-percent joking.

I'm with you on that. You also really like basketball, right? Who's your favorite player of all-time?

This answer isn't gonna be funny, but Allen Iverson is both my favorite NBA player of all time, and the biggest inspiration in my life. I grew up in Philadelphia, and the Sixers' 2001 playoff run is still one of the all-time best times in my life. When Iverson hit that step back jumper over Tyronn Lue and stepped over him in game one of the finals, I was convinced the Sixers were going to win in four games. Of course, they lost in five. Typical Philly shit.

Even though Iverson never won a championship, and you could argue he never lived up to his full potential, he was and still is an inspiration to me. The adversity he overcame, his stubborn individuality, his flaws, his sense of humor, his vulnerability, his openness... it has all informed who I am today.

I have this idea that everyone has like five or so people in the world that have informed who they are, like a vision board of people that make up their personality. If I actually maintained a vision board, Allen Iverson would be the most visible person. I can't really explain it, but I don't think I would be the man I am today without having grown up in Philly with Iverson as my favorite player. Not only is he the best little man to ever play the game, he's a guy that overcame incredible odds--on his own terms--to become a hall of fame player. He's my hero.

Why do you think comedians become comedians?

I'd call myself a comedy writer and not a comedian. Strictly speaking for myself, the reason why I became a comedy writer is that it's the only thing I've ever done that I'm both very good at and makes me happy.

What are you working on now?

I've got a couple of projects that I actually can't talk about right now. Talk to me in a month, I should be able to say what they are then.

What makes a joke funny?

Go look at my Twitter page and you'll see I have no idea.

WRITERS

YASSIR LESTER

@Yassir_Lester

Yassir is a stand-up comic who has written for HBO's Girls and NBC's The Carmichael Show. He has also appeared on Comedy Central's Key and Peele, MTV's Guy Code and will co-star on FOX's Making History.

Where did you grow up?

I lived in a lot of places but I consider my home to be Marietta, Georgia.

What's interesting or uninteresting about Marietta?

It's completely uninteresting on paper. There's really nothing about it that would make someone want to go there. But beneath the surface of ordinary and sterile, there is a subculture of segregation and drug abuse and dark family secrets.

It's very much like every indie movie of the early 2000s where a small suburban community is filled with darkness. Like Donnie Darko or that other terrible movie the Chumscrubber. Or American Beauty.

What did your parents do for a living when you were a kid?

My mom did many jobs. Usually office work. My dad bailed so I have no idea what he did. Except maybe get other women pregnant.

What was the first bit you tried onstage?

The first joke I ever did was about me snorting dollar bills because they had traces of drugs on them. Closing bit was about me getting a prostate exam so I was praying I died before forty.

When and/or where did you figure out you could be a comedian?

I always knew I could be and always wanted to be. Probably decided at 14-years-old subconsciously that's what I wanted to do. Didn't pull the trigger 'til age 19 though when I did my first open mic. Didn't actually start doing stand-up for real until age 24.

How did you start writing for Girls on HBO? What's different about their creation process?

I was blessed enough to be suggested to write on a pilot called "Brothers in Atlanta" for HBO by Adult Swim Executive Producer Walter Newman, a dude who I owe more than I can even fathom. While working on that pilot I met an executive producer on Girls named Murray Miller (writer of HBO's "7 Days in Hell"), who I owe my firstborn child. He introduced me to Jenni Konner and Lena Dunham, who are two of the most perfect people I've ever met and we hit it off. Then they offered me a job.

I know it sounds like hyperbole, but all of the people I mentioned above are truly geniuses and the fact that I've been given the opportunity to work with any of them is huge. Make sure that you pay attention to the people you work with. Their habits, their style, etc. and emulate it. Or realize it's the opposite of what you want and do your own thing.

MTV seems to really embrace young comedians. What are they doing that other networks are missing?

Giving comics a chance. But MTV is also a machine like anything else. They constantly need to bring in new talent because of their formatting of shows. There's 30 comics on each episode of Guy/Girl Code. All their shows run 20 times a day. If they didn't bring in new talent you'd see five faces on that channel for 23-hours-a-day.

What do you like or dislike about comedy in New York?

I love NYC comedy in its diversity. LA, though disguised as a liberal comedy community is quite the opposite. If bookers weren't forced, there would be no minorities of any kinds on any shows. It's a conscious choice to have people of color, women, and LGBT comics on the show lineups. In NYC, comics are booked on the strength of their set. That being said, for as highly regarded as NYC comics seem to hold their comedy out here, to me, it seems to be quite homogeneous. Lotta the same topics discussed. Comics feeling the need to work ultra-dirty.

In the same way NY comics say LA comedy is all based on act outs, NY comedy is trying its hardest to be dirty just because the general attitude here is "we're a rougher city" when in fact it's not. There's barely any crime. It's the face of gentrification. So I think NY comics rely on a false reputation instead of trying to do something different.

How did The Block Comic originate? What do you enjoy about illustration?

The Block was an idea I literally came up with in a pitch packet to a major comic publisher. They never responded. I asked my friend if he wanted to write it with me. He said yes.

I found an artist off Twitter. I decided to sink money into it knowing I would lose a ton, but at least I was doing something that was fun and made me happy and was a dream fulfillment.

Why do some jokes work on the internet and others don't?

Some jokes work because people are smart. Some jokes don't work because people are stupid.

Who is the funniest person you know?

I know a ton of comics so that's hard. I mean, Chelsea Peretti is legitimately one of the funniest people on the planet, easily. I laugh so hard at pretty much everything she says. Her brain operates on a level that most people would be afraid of even approaching within themselves, but she lets herself go. She's amazing. But then on the opposite end of the spectrum are Lena and Jenni. Like Jenni is so sly. And Lena knows what to write for characters' dialogue that make them these insane hilarious people to watch. Chrissy Teigen is kind of outta her mind, and can crack me up just by speaking her mind. My Mom Vicki is a silly lady and can always make me laugh. She's too real and it's hilarious. And my brother Isaiah, who is a phenomenal writer, is so funny it's crazy that he doesn't do standup. Like he's great.

But a ton of people I know are funny. It's different with different people. Comedians Robby Slowik and Casey Balsham are super funny. Akaash Singh and Rell Battle are funny. Johnny Skourtis and Josh Adam Meyers are funny. Reza Riazi is funny. Brittany my sister is funny. Comedian Nore Davis. I don't know. Jerrod Carmichael and Jamar Neighbors are funny. Janelle James, Tracy Clayton, Heben Nigatu, Aeysha Carr, and Justine Marino are funny. Garrick Bernard and Jak Knight are funny.

Why are jokes funny?

Because I'm literally a genius.

MORGAN EVANS

@totallymorgan

Morgan is a writer, actor, producer and director known for The Untitled Web Series That Morgan Evans is Doing for MTV, Best Week Ever, The Onion and Disconnected.

What was the first bit or joke you performed on stage?

The first "joke" I remember writing and putting on its feet was: "I'm always thinking about sex or death. If I'm not thinking about sex, I'm thinking about death. If I'm not thinking about death, I'm thinking about sex. If I'm not thinking of either it's because I'm hanging myself and jerking off at the same time."

Ehhhhh. It did OK.

Where did you grow up?

I am originally from Mesa, Arizona.

What's interesting or uninteresting about Mesa?

I always say Arizona is like Los Angeles with even less of a culture, but I guess now that I look back on it, that's unfair to say. Arizona was great because it had this INSANE music scene in Phoenix so I was able to get tons of stage time very young.

I would perform in joke bands and do comedy bits at punk and noise shows pretty much non-stop since I was 12. Without places in Phoenix like The Trunkspace, Four White Walls, The Phix, etc. I don't know if I would have had the confidence to keep attempting comedy.

What did your parents do for a living when you were a kid?

My dad is an insurance agent and my mom was a stay at home mom. Before that she was a flight attendant. She's also the greatest cook of all time.

You write and direct a ton of content with MTV. It seems like they allow you to create freely. How did that relationship begin?

I was working at The Onion for about three years while I was in college, which was a very lucky experience. I was hired as an intern originally and then moved my way up and became Segment Producer on the IFC show. They ended up moving the company to Chicago and I wasn't going to go with them — so I quit and went off and created my own web series that did alright; it got nominated for a WGA award and screened at some festivals in New York. Through that, I think a few people at MTV saw it and decided to meet with me. I pitched them a show called "Teachers' Lounge," which they bought, and then we ended up making stuff together for about three years.

What's an important lesson you've learned about directing?

Don't be afraid to take advice from other people.

Don't let your ego get in the way. If you surround yourself with smart, hilarious, people, you'll end up with a great product if you know what to say yes to. If the grip has the funniest idea you've heard all day, why not shoot it?

What do you like or dislike about comedy in New York?

I love New York's comedy scene. Mostly because people are working their asses off and constantly putting stuff on stage, shooting, etc. What I don't like about it is that it seems to have been co-opted by the Buzzfeed/HuffPo mentality of listicle, click bait, "Hey that's topical let's shoot it," viral video, bullshit. It makes me upset and I think it's a waste of time.

Who is the funniest person you know?

My best friend since childhood, Tim Mahoney, is hands down the funniest guy I have ever met and probably ever will meet. He will do bits that last seven hours and completely fry your brain. He's like Andy Kaufman and Letterman rolled into Daniel Day Lewis.

Who is the funniest person you don't know?

I think Jack Handey is very funny. I think Albert Brooks is very funny. I think Charles Grodin is severely underrated.

Why are jokes funny?

"According to Marx, repetition is comic when it falls short–that is, when instead of leading to metamorphosis and the production of something new, it forms a kind of involution, the opposite of an authentic creation." —Deleuze

Or, you know, poop.

AMANDA ROSENBERG

🐦 *@AmandaRosenberg*

Amanda is a comedy writer and British werewolf in San Francisco. She is a feminist monster, mental health advocate and mostly a blanket. Her comedy has been seen on Killing My Lobster, McSweeney's, Slackjaw on Medium, The Hairpin and HBO's Silicon Valley (contributor).

Where did you grow up?

I grew up in London, England.

What's interesting or uninteresting about London?

We have free healthcare and 'pudding' is an umbrella term for dessert.

When and why did you first start writing comedy?

As is the law in the UK, I grew up watching a lot of Monty Python. So, from a young age, I was writing Python-esque sketches, which turned out to be truly awful— surreal —but awful.

Also, I have a gross compulsion to make people laugh/like me.

How did Grown Ass Woman come together? What is your creation process for the series?

They say 'write what you know' and I only know how to be a woman in her late-twenties who's still trying to get her shit together. I met Alli Zamani (who also writes and stars in Grown Ass Woman's 'Apartment' series) through a sketch group we were part of. When I pitched her the idea, she related to a lot of the themes—not having enough energy to go out, feeling the pressure of not being as successful as you'd thought you'd be at this age, etc. We film in a very fast, disorganized way because I'm impatient and have delusions of Robert Rodriguez-esque grandeur.

Typically, once we've written the script, we'll shoot on Saturday and start editing straightaway which means we can post the following week. This is all made possible by our director, Marcus Stenbeck.

Can you talk about writing for Killing My Lobster? What do you enjoy most about sketch comedy?

Killing My Lobster is a sketch comedy…I wanna say 'troupe' but then I really don't wanna say 'troupe'…who I write for. They are based in San Francisco and put on a live sketch show every month. Putting on a show every month means you have to be smart, fast, and fearless with your writing which can be both grueling and exhilarating at the same time. That said, KML is the best, and I am fortunate to be able to work with the funniest writers and actors IN THE WORLD.

What do I enjoy most about sketch comedy? The pace and the distillation—there's no room for filler in a sketch. For me, the best sketches are those that heighten everyday situations in an unpredictable and absurd way, which is probably why Monty Python's 'Four Yorkshiremen' is one of my favorite sketches of all time.

How did you end up getting cast as Jason Statham in a play? What is the play going to be about?

I think it's because I'm British but I defer to Allison Page, the writer of the play:

"JASONS is a play about every famous Jason retelling the story of Jason & The Argonauts in order to show that Jasons are still relevant, because the world is now run by Kaedens and Madysons with a Y in the middle. It was written for the San Francisco Olympians Festival which is a new works festival based on Greek mythology. Amanda is so obviously Jason Statham I can't even understand why anyone would ask that question. She's clearly an action star and, though I haven't seen this first hand, I would assume she looks pretty kickass with a shaved head. The Olympians Festival pulls in around 150 auditioners each year, and this is the first time I've pulled someone in who didn't come to auditions. When a Statham speaks to you, you must answer the call and pull some strings. Also, she's just really funny."

Is it more difficult to be a female comedy writer?

Yes, because of questions like this.

What do you like or dislike about comedy in San Francisco?

I like the sense of community. The comedy scene in San Francisco is (relatively) not as sprawling as LA or New York. It feels more inclusive.

Who is the funniest person you know?

My brother, who is neither a comedian, nor is he involved in comedy in any way. The thing that makes me laugh the most is watching him laugh at something I don't find funny at all. Then when he explains why he finds it funny, it just makes me laugh even more.

Why are jokes funny?

Jokes all have a kernel of truth to them.

A truth, no matter how dark, crude, or shameful, that we can all relate to. When we laugh at a joke it's an expression of relief, like "thank fuck someone else said what I was thinking".

CHELSEA DAVISON

🐦 *@chelsea_davison*

Chelsea is a cast member on the upcoming MADtv reboot on the CW and couldn't be more excited! Before MADtv, Chelsea was a staff writer on the show *@midnight* on Comedy Central, and wrote on the comedy game show *Lie Detectors*. She performs stand-up, improv, and sketch comedy all over town, with solo shows at the UCB Theater in NY, and appearances at The Stand, Broadway Comedy Club, Flappers, The Nerdmelt Showroom, and more. She was also named a "New Face" at the 2014 Just For Laughs Festival in Montreal, and was chosen as one of five writers or to participate in the 2014 NBC Late Night Writers Workshop.

Where did you grow up?

I'm from Cleveland, Ohio.

What's interesting or uninteresting about Cleveland?

It's historically been a city of disappointment (our sports teams and our economy are often abysmal) so you have to have a sense of humor about things.

What do your parents do for a living?

My dad is a pilot and my mom does commercial real estate.

What was the first joke or bit that you tried onstage?

I compared one-night stands to eating Peeps—you think it'll be fun, but you always end up sticky and feeling sick.

When (or where) did you realize you could write for a living?

In college I got a job as a blogger. It only paid $10/article but I was thrilled to be getting paid for something I enjoyed doing (my other part-time job at the time was selling strollers). After that I pursued writing in advertising, which is just as fun but pays much better. Comedy writing was another step away, but by that time I at least knew I could be paid to write.

The NBC Late Night Writers Workshop sounds like a grueling, rewarding process. How do they prepare young creatives?

Unlike some of the other writing fellowships, the NBC Late Night Writers Workshop is actually pretty relaxed! It's only a few days long, where we workshop various aspects of late night shows and packets. It's really fun and a great way to sharpen your skills writing monologue jokes, desk pieces, and sketches.

Also, it's a great first taste of a writers room.

What's the origin story behind "Sex? Who Needs It!" at UCB?

I write and perform characters and so wanted a way to showcase my favorite pieces in one 30-minute solo show. The UCB was amazing and let me put it up there, which taught me a lot. I ended up rewriting it after and putting it up at the PIT.

Based on what I learned from that show, I'm going to rewrite it again and put it up out in Los Angeles.

Do you especially enjoy competition television?

No, I think game shows can be fun but I really enjoy writing jokes. It just happened to work out that the first gig I got was a game show, and @midnight is a game show in the same way The Daily Show is a news show—that's the show's structure, but it's the comedy that keeps you there.

How did you begin writing for @midnight?

I submitted a packet in 2014, while the show was looking for a new head writer. I didn't hear anything, so in the meantime took a job writing on 'Lie Detectors.' Shortly after 'Lie Detectors' ended, our head writer was named the head writer of @midnight. I reached out to see if I could resubmit a packet, knowing this time it would get read, and he generously agreed.

Our show is different because it combines formats to make a really unique news-oriented panel show. It's a great blend of silly and serious, and incredibly fast-paced. Also, from a behind-the-scenes standpoint, it's a really supportive writers room.

How does the New York comedy scene compare with the Los Angeles comedy scene?

I only just moved to L.A. so I don't think I can answer this! However, the New York comedy scene is really amazing. It's huge and yet very tightly knit.

I'm hoping L.A.'s comedy scene will be similar!

Who is the funniest person you know?

That's hard to answer because different people make me laugh in different contexts. On Twitter Michelle Wolf (@michelleisawolf) cracks me up with jokes. At shows, I'm always captivated by what John Early (@bejohnce) does. Watching improv is always better when Brennan Lee Mulligan (@BrennanLM) is on stage.

And in our writers room it's impossible not to crack up when Blaine Capatch (@blainecapatch) does a bit. I'm lucky enough to be around a lot of really funny people.

Why are jokes funny?

It depends!

Oh man, I took a humor theory class at NYU all about this. It's usually some combination of a recognizable truth + something subversive + an unexpected surprise + timing.

MIKE GLAZER

🐦 *@glazerboohoohoo*

Mike is a writer and comedian whose work has been featured on BuzzFeed, Food Network, FUSE, truTV, Funny or Die, Second City and UCB. He is always writing.

Where did you grow up?

I grew up in St. Louis, moved to Chicago, and am currently in Los Angeles.

What's interesting or uninteresting about St. Louis?

St. Louis is fine. Good place to grow up and learn how to be a person. Hockey was my life. I'm a goalie, and it was all I cared about. Hockey and comedy. That was it. I'm lucky to have some success in both after doing them a very long time.

Where did you first perform comedy?

My first memory of performing was for my babysitter Rebecca. I would run full speed across our wood floor, slip on a foam mat, and fall on my face...prat falls, repeatedly. I had her in tears.

She couldn't stop laughing at me fall over and over. Sometimes I'd switch it up, and instead of running full speed I'd pretend I didn't see the mat and trip onto it face first. We had a great night.

What was the first bit you tried onstage?

My first set was at the St. Louis Funny Bone open mic. It was about parents telling their kids not to talk to strangers, but then hiring clowns to do their kid's birthday party, and NOTHING is stranger than a clown. You don't even know what a clown looks like, their face is covered in makeup and they can fit three kids in their parachute pants so why are they talking to your children?

Talk about writing for Billy on the Street. How did you come up with topics for the show?

That was one of the funniest writing packets I've ever submitted. I remember getting an email from something else saying I didn't get the job, and I was disappointed. The next day a Billy On The Street producer called saying they liked my packet. Vindication! To write the BOTS packet I went to Walgreens, bought every celebrity magazine, and just started writing jokes based on them. It was great.

Those yak voicemails are hilarious. What was your motivation behind that project? What do you enjoy most about prank art?

I love pranks. I'm obsessed with them. From an early age. I think it started with learning magic, tricking people, then eventually I just cut out the magic part to get to trickery faster. What I love about pranks is that they give people a better day. Pranks give them something memorable to talk about around the dinner table with their family, or at the bar with their friends. Pranks shake it up, and shaking it up is the most important thing we can do for ourselves and others.

I think the best part about the Lost Yak flyers is using social media to touch more people than I expected. The people who left insane voicemails on my cell phone were great. They are fun people who like to play (except the head of the neighborhood who threatened to call the cops), but everyone else was cool. I was impressed when I went on Instagram and saw post after post at

#LOSTYAK of people laughing and sharing it with their friends. A flyer I made as a prank reached across the country and Europe and that's really cool.

Why do some jokes work on the internet and others don't?

I don't know why some work and others don't, but I know the more you write the better your odds of finding good ones.

Who is the funniest person you know?

One of the funniest people I know on Twitter is @home_halfway. Also, Lindsay Monahan. She's the sharpest funniest person I know. Her physical and verbal comedy are untouchable, effortless. Plus, she's an incredible costume designer...a natural artist.

Why are jokes funny?

Jokes are funny because life is ridiculous.

JON SAVITT

@savittj

Jon is a writer, journalist, comedian and twenty-something who talks about napping the way rappers talk about money. He has spent time writing for TIME, MTV News, The Huffington Post, Paste Magazine, Thought Catalog, BuzzFeed, Funny or Die and more.

What's your name and where did you grow up?

My name is Jon Savitt, I'm 23, and I grew up in St. Louis Park, MN (a suburb of Minneapolis). After attending college at Indiana University I moved back to Minneapolis—where I have been living since. It's only like Antarctica sometimes.

What was the first bit or joke you submit that was published?

Oh god. It's funny, I remember this perfectly. I was a sophomore in college when I had my first article published. I think I was supposed to be studying for a final or something and got sidetracked (but studying is important and school is good). It was a satirical article about how to play guitar, the benefits, and why you should learn—essentially talking about how it's not important to actually be skilled, rather it's about making sure you bring your guitar to college and to bonfires, know how to play some John Mayer, etc. College Humor published the article and that was a big motivating factor in terms of me continuing to write.

It got like 10, maybe even 12 "likes" on Facebook, so yeah, I was kind of a big deal.

What advice would you give someone trying to get his or her work published?

Alright, here's my number one piece of advice, and it's nothing crazy. It's nothing groundbreaking. It's nothing revolutionary. Be persistent. When I was younger and inexperienced and less handsome I had the pleasure of talking with a lot of successful comedians and writers: from actors on TV to writers on The Daily Show to screenwriters; and everyone would tell me this. Usually, I would say thank you and move on not fully understanding or believing in their words—thinking it was just the first thing that popped into their head.

But then I committed to the idea of being persistent and working hard and it changed everything. Regarding every site you mentioned (and more)—I started off by being rejected many times. It took me months of emails, phone calls, and meetings to land the MTV gig. It's important to understand that in an industry like this often times you see the success, but you fail to see the effort that got there—I think that's true a lot in life. Listen carefully to the feedback you receive and try to improve every day you wake up. Be polite and keep in touch with those you have contacted, even if they rejected you, you never know if they'll love your next article.

And never be afraid to take initiative or ask a question. It never hurts. Sometimes my opportunities simply came from emailing a magazine or website and saying, "Hey, I have this idea for an article or a column, mind if I give it a shot?" and sometimes that works. But you have to be proactive. OK, that was a lot. Maybe I should write an advice book.

Do you really want to be on The Bachelor?

Yes! I was absolutely serious about that. Couldn't you tell? I think I spent more time on that application than I did studying for the ACT back in the day. Unless my parents are reading this then I studied a lot. But, yeah, my whole thing was that I believe relationships, for the most part, are being represented unrealistically or simply absurdly on reality television.

And even furthermore from what I was seeing with people around me—lying on dating profiles, changing things about themselves to impress their love interest, I was sensing a lot of self-consciousness, so I kinda wanted to publicly put myself out there as if to say: I'm real, I'm awkward, I'm unapologetic, and I'm here to find love. But I guess ABC wasn't really feeling that. That's okay though, I don't know if you saw or not, but I wrote them a follow up email after not being selected. I think I got the last laugh.

Any thoughts on the Republican presidential nominees? Does this whole process start too early?

Yeah. I have thoughts. I have a lot of thoughts. It's to the point where I honestly just think politics in our country is laughable. From the entertainment-driven debates to the talk show appearances to candidate "Deez Nuts" gaining support, it's laughable. But in the worst way. Like the kind of laugh that turns into a cry and then I go drown myself in french fries and then move to Canada. That kind of laugh.

You seem to really like tweeting at big companies. What kind of kick do you get out of when they respond?

I get a bigger kick than I probably should. I'll tell you that much. The people that run those social media accounts are the true heroes. They get sooo many complaints per day and have to put up with so much negativity that I really just want to provide them with some spontaneity, a little excitement, and hopefully a laugh. It's really great when they indulge and come back with something creative, though.

One time I asked American Airlines how to flirt with someone sitting next to me on the plane, they gave me advice and played along. Another time I asked Chili's if they would cater my eventual funeral, they didn't particularly like that. I just think life should be fun and not be taken too seriously.

Do you prefer forming jokes on paper or on stage?

There is beauty in both forms. There are things I write on paper that could only be delivered and understood in such a way, and then there are jokes and stories that really only come to life through words. Though the two overlap, there's really no such feeling as connecting with a crowd through laughter and emotion, bringing them in as part of the story, and feeling that energy, at the same time I'll always have that love for sitting down and writing. So I didn't really answer that question. I just like jokes, okay?

Who is the funniest person you know?

I try to surround myself with as many funny people as possible. I love to laugh. That being said, this is easy, it's my brother. He's funnier than me. He's so quick. I run a lot of my material by him. You should be interviewing him instead. I can give you his number.

ALISON LEIBY

🐦 *@AlisonLeiby*

Alison is a writer and stand-up in New York City. Her work has been featured in The New York Times, The Huffington Post, Eater, New York Mag, McSweeny's and Medium. Her TV writing credits include "We Have Issues" on E! and the Triumph The Insult Comic Dog's Convention Special.

What did your parents do for a living when you were a kid?

My mom was an English teacher, which is part of why I ended up in comedy—I was raised by someone who also loves to tell people when they're wrong. My dad had a lot of executive level jobs in what I can only really categorize as "business" (I'm in my 30s and still don't quite understand the world outside of the arts). He's good at managing people, which resulted in lots of mind games when I was growing up.

> They were the fun kind that are now great stories and the basis of bits for me, not like, the kind that land you in five-days-a-week therapy for life.

Where did you grow up?

Severna Park, MD.

What's life like in Severna Park?

Severna Park is a pretty basic suburb. Chain restaurants, high school sports, the usual. As much as I enjoyed those things when I lived there, I never fully felt like I fit in. I think that was mostly because I'm Jewish, and our entire town was populated by blonde, attractive Christian kids. It kind of felt like going to school with hundreds of golden retrievers that believed in Jesus and didn't appreciate sarcasm.

Why did you first want to start performing comedy? What was the first joke or bit you tried on stage?

I've loved stand-up for as long as I can remember, but I didn't know you could just, like, do it. When I was 26 and bored by my job, I decided to start doing some storytelling in the city. I had survived a horrific surgical complication a few years before and I wanted to talk or write about it. When I started putting together the story, I kept returning to the parts of the experience that I found funny. I ended this super dramatic account of almost dying with a punchline about a very dumb tattoo I have, and then I realized, "I guess stand-up would just be doing this but without the long sad parts about being in a hospital." I still tell that story a few times a year, though, and I still love it.

Do you prefer forming jokes on paper or on stage?

I prefer writing jokes on paper and thinking them through a lot. I've had a handful of jokes that I have written on stage in the moment (including my only cum joke!), but on the whole I write things out pretty thoroughly.

What do you like or dislike about comedy in New York?

My deep love for New York probably influences how I feel about the comedy scene. I'm the kind of person who is like, "The man who pisses on my front steps every morning told me I looked nice today! I love this city!"

But I think doing comedy in New York is just as good as it gets. There's so much to interact with and so much to comment on here that you're just constantly writing and thinking even when you aren't trying to. When a weird five-foot-tall man kisses your bare upper arm on a crowded subway, what are you going to do? Just like, not turn that into a bit? That's insane.

You and Alyssa Wolff are a kind of dynamic writing duo. How did you two meet? Why did you want to start writing parody books?

Dynamic writing duo, inseparable comedy monsters, whatever you want to call it. A few years ago we had each been doing stand-up for a little while, crossed paths at open mics, but didn't really know each other. Then Alyssa booked me on a show she was running. I got there and we chatted for a minute and immediately learned that we're both nightmares who went to Ivy League schools and constantly tried to hide it from other comics—which then only made us look worse.

After bonding over that embarrassing fact, we did the next logical thing and each drank four glasses of red wine for dinner to solidify our new best friend status. Two weeks later we were sharing a hotel room at the Bridgetown Comedy Festival and saying how we should work on something together. We're feminists and had each worked in book publishing before comedy, so we were familiar with Sheryl Sandberg's Lean In. Writing a parody of that book was a no-brainer. We finished it within weeks. It did well and got a lot of attention. Once we saw how easy it was for us to write something together, we ran with it and did another parody book a year later in addition to dozens of humor pieces for everyone from Marie Claire to McSweeney's. Right now we're working on some bigger projects when we're not having wine dinner, obviously.

Do you think it's harder for women to break into professional comedy? If so- why? If not- why not?

Only on the days that we're menstruating!

What's the last thing you Google searched?

A restaurant menu. I would say that 80 percent of my Google searches are for menus, 15 percent are researching serial killers, and 5 percent are "Alison Leiby hot" (which never yields the results I'm looking for)

Who is the funniest person you know?

My parents. No question.

Why are jokes funny?

I love all kinds of jokes.

They are probably my favorite thing on Earth besides chips and rolling my eyes at people. They're great because they can make you laugh at something that you shouldn't necessarily laugh at. In some cases, that's something dark or difficult. In other cases, that's something boring or mundane. But the fact that I have laughed equally as hard at a rape joke as I have at a joke about carrots proves that they can be about anything and serve their purpose.

The surprise of finding something funny in things that are inherently humorless is what makes them so exciting.

BRENDAN MCLAUGHLIN

@btmclaughlin

Brendan is a stand-up comedian and writer living in New York City. He's written for VH1's Best Week Ever, truTV's Almost Genius and MTV's Nikki & Sara Live, and has contributed content for Comedy Central, IFC and MTV2. In 2016 he was named one of the 50 Funniest People in Brooklyn by Brooklyn Magazine. He performs stand-up at venues all over the city, including the Upright Citizens Brigade Theatre and Caroline's on Broadway. He enjoys The Replacements.

When did you realize you could write and perform comedy?

I think just as a kid I'd watch Seinfeld and Saturday Night Live and think, 'That's those people's jobs. I want to do that.' And then later I started having comedian friends getting hired for this and that and thinking, 'Hey, they're in my comedy world and now they're doing that. I could probably do that too. What were they doing that got them that job that I'm NOT doing?' The answer was just writing a lot and being funny. It took me several years to figure that out.

Where did you grow up?

I grew up in Havertown, PA, a suburb of Philadelphia. I lied about the Steenburgen.

What's cool about Havertown?

I think there's a certain sense of humor unique to that area. My friends from growing up are hilarious, and I can't tell you how many times I've met someone and hit it off with them immediately, then found out they're from somewhere around Philly. Maybe it's just that we're all assholes… also Tina Fey is from one town over from me and we went to the same theater camp (at different times). I remember the camp director announcing, "A former Summer Stager is now a writer at Saturday Night Live—Tina Fey," and thinking, 'Who the hell is that? I've never heard of her. She must not be a big deal.'

What did your parents do for a living when you were a kid?

My dad's a salesman in the car industry and my mom is a "fixer" for the U.S. government. Just kidding. She's a teacher.

What were the sequence of events that led to you becoming a writer on VH1's Best Week Ever?

I had written on Nikki & Sara Live for two seasons and a little while after that heard Best Week Ever was taking packets. I submitted a packet, had a meeting with the head writer and executive producers and got the job. As I write this I realize, this story is boring.

What did you enjoy most about writing for Nikki and Sara Live?

The people. Nikki and Sara are great and were a blast to work for. I got to work for Brian McCann who I grew up watching on Late Night with Conan, which remains one of my favorite shows ever. Also, I got along great with the rest of the writing staff, which included Emmy Blotnick, Gabe Gronli, Chase Mitchell, Justin Shanes and others. We had a blast together and I learned a ton from them (except for Chase).

How did Let Me Save You Some Time come about? Why do you want to save people time?

I saw the movie Inherent Vice and while I didn't hate it, I just didn't think it was worth sitting through. The next day I was bitching about it to a friend on GChat, and I came up with the idea. I might have even said, "Let me save you some time. The whole movie is just blah blah blah." I had wanted to do something with no production value that I could just crank out quickly, and thought complaining about things I didn't enjoy could be a decent vehicle for my comedy. I opened another GChat window and asked my friend Andrew Ciesla if he could make a little intro with my head spinning out and sync it with a horrible one chord theme song I was about to create (it's an A chord for any fans looking to cover it!). He made the awesome intro that same day, and the first episode was done hours later. It was very fast and efficient—and I've been slow and lazy about it ever since.

Do you prefer forming jokes on paper or on stage? Why?

I kind of do both and also neither. I tend to mostly come up with things in my head and/or by talking them out with my friends. When I write stuff down it's usually bullet points just so I won't forget what I came up with. If I write something out all the way it's often to email it to a friend and say, "Is this funneh???" And then they write back and say, "No."

Then when I do it onstage I'll try different things with it, or in many cases come up with some line on the spot that's funnier than all the lines I agonized over and feel like a jackass. For some reason with writing in general I like to have a lot of the idea in my head already before I sit down with a notebook or at a computer. You can't always do that though. My life is VERY difficult.

The newest James Bond film, Spectre, is likely the most expensive film ever made ($300m?). What do you think that says about the movie industry today?

I'm a giant Bond fan and whiner so I'm fine with this. Generally, I'm ok with big budget movies as long as I feel like the people behind them gave a shit about making them good. I did feel that way about Spectre. I enjoyed it. It's pretty impossible to top Skyfall because: a) it was just a great movie and b) Javier Bardem was, for my money, the best main villain in the history of the series (I'm not counting henchmen).

So the fact that Spectre continued the good stuff that was set up in the last one—and even built on those things—resulted in me leaving the theater with a smile on my face and a slight boner. I just think Daniel Craig and Sam Mendes get what things make a good Bond movie and genuinely tried to make something that fans of the series would love. Jesus, I am a whiner. I get annoyed by bad writing in movies—or more specifically, lazy writing—where I feel like the team behind the movie assumed their audience would be stupid and not notice that the script they're working off of is dog shit. I felt that way about movies like X3, The Man From U.N.C.L.E., Russell Crowe's Robin Hood, and other things that I've forgotten about because they were so unmemorable…

It does seem like everything's a reboot or remake these days and that's getting old. Is the growing popularity of huge movies making it harder for smaller movies to get made and seen? I honestly don't know because I don't go around trying to get films made. If that is happening, I think it's bad. At the same time, I've seen shitty smaller movies too. I don't think the budget of the movie is the main thing, but rather—does it blow?

What do you like or dislike about comedy in New York?

I like that there are so, so many hilarious and talented people. On any given night you can go see great comedians—well known or not—do stand-up, sketch or improv. I've made a lot of hilarious friends through comedy here, which is great because hilarious friends are a good thing to have, and also I have all these people that I run ideas by and learn from.

I don't like that I've only done one show this year where there's been free cheese and charcuterie backstage for me to snack on. The biggest problem with comedy right now is a shortage of charcuterie. I also don't like that audiences didn't get on board with the Frasier joke I tried to bring into the rotation a few months back...

Who is the funniest person you know?

I'm very lucky in that I know a lot of funny people. They're the only people I want to know, but they're not, unfortunately. It would take too long to name everybody. I'm super lucky I got to work for Brian McCann. He's just as hilarious in person as he was on Conan and all the other things he's done, and he's just a cool guy. My Uncle Zeke is really fucking funny as is my sister Kelsey. My dad is funny too, and also invaluable in that he's inadvertently provided me with lots of stand-up material.

Why are jokes funny?

Because I said so.

KENNY DUCEY

@KennyDucey

Kenny is a writer for Sports Illustrated and Baseball Prospectus. He was once a freelance reporter with Metro Networks, the Associated Press, and CBS Sports Radio. He is also a Fordham grad.

Where did you grow up?

I grew up in Ridgefield, Connecticut.

What's interesting or uninteresting about Ridgefield?

It's a nice little town, but there's not too much that's incredibly interesting about it.

Paul Revere once rode through. There's a dope homemade chocolate place on Main Street that's been there for a while. French Montana used to play shows in Danbury, where I went to high school. It's like 15 minutes north of town.

What do your parents do for a living?

They're both currently running a startup called HamletHub, which is sort of like a Bleacher Report for local news.

They're in over 50 towns now. There's an editor in each town who runs a blog for their town and posts about businesses and events in stuff. So my mother does that in town & oversees the larger operation as well.

What interested you about sports writing as a child?

Like a lot of people that I speak to in the industry, I didn't want to be in the media as a kid. I wanted to be on the field—that was always the dream. I can't tell you why I love sports so much or when I became interested. All I can remember is the first time my dad taught me how to field grounders. I was like "nah man I'm out, this is too hard." Next thing you know, I went to baseball camp, I joined a soccer team, and I got ice skating lessons. I think I played every sport as a kid.

As I was doing all this, the Yankees were absolutely killing it. I remember some of the '96 World Series, believe it or not (I was only three). I had the '98-season on VHS. I watched that entire tape at least twice a week—it was ridiculous. But the more I learned more about the sport, the more I wanted to watch that season. I remember Michael Kay calling Tino Martinez's Grand Slam in Game 1 of the World Series. I think that sort of planted some sort of seed in me that I wanted to share sports with as many people as possible, and play-by-play would be a cool way to do that. That always sort of seemed to be my second dream job after playing in the bigs.

It just grew as I got older realized I was gonna grow up to be 5' 10" with a slim build.

Did you write in college? If so, where? What did you cover?

In junior year, I wrote columns for the Fordham Ram. That was the extent of my traditional college journalism experience. The non-traditional part was working at WFUV. No school in the country has what that station has. Being an NPR affiliate, we were credentialed to cover every pro sports team in New York, in addition to any big event in town. The US Open (both tennis and golf), the Super Bowl, drafts, etc... we were there.

It wasn't in my job description there, but I wrote a lot for our website from those games. They were often columns, bits of news, or statistical breakdowns. I wrote a bunch of stuff there, I wrote, produced, and voiced radio features, I did play-by-play, talk shows, updates, producing, literally everything there was to do. I made connections going to those games and earned some more work outside of FUV—that's where the freelance radio stuff and some of the pieces I've done for other sites come in to play. So in short, I covered pro sports in school on WFUV's website, with some work on the side.

What do you cover with Baseball Prospectus?

I exclusively write about the Yankees at Prospectus. They've expanded this year and added local sites for a few teams, and that's where I come in. I use BP's extensive database of stats to look deep into the team's trends, and blend that with a bit of reporting by asking players and coaches about them. I really like it there and like the ideas of the local sites—their coverage was all-encompassing, but of course had some limits before the smaller sites were born. Now, you can read about a specific reliever in the Yankees' bullpen, or something like that.

What do you do at SI?

I write about baseball, basketball and breaking news for the site, with some off-beat stuff mixed in at our Extra Mustard page.

Why do some tweets hit and others don't?

That's the million-dollar question that no one seems to have the answer to. The thing about Twitter is that if you've built up a solid follower base (maybe 20,000 or more), basically anything you tweet is going to get engagement. When you're in that sort of 2,000–10,000 range like I am, it's up and down. You've always got to be on top of your game. In a way, it makes your tweets better, really. In an event like the NBA Finals, for example, I won't tweet unless I have something that I think is quality.

It's just about not over-doing it and trying to keep as many tweets as possible quality. That said, people sort of look upon you to tweet during events like that if you're an established part of the NBA twitter community. So, it's a challenge. I just think you have to keep punchlines short, and know your followers. Pop culture references are key, but in my case, so are basketball references. I guess you just have to have a lot of useless knowledge like on deck. It also helps to have big accounts following you. If you tweet good tweets, they will follow, and they will Retweet. That's usually how tweets hit.

Technology-wise, where is the future of sports reporting headed?

Everything is going digital, and it's moving to real-time, as many have started to see. Twitter is where an increasing number of sports fans go for real-time updates on games, injuries, and more. It might not be Twitter necessarily, but there's going to be a stress on social networks, wherever they head. I do think there will be more fun stuff, like I mentioned, mixed in.

You have to differentiate yourself if you want to be successful. To write stories like that is to humanize these athletes and connect them with fans.

Who is the most underrated NBA point guard of the past 15 seasons?

I think I'm actually gonna go with Baron Davis. He played a lot of games until he got to the Knicks (over 12 years). And his numbers weren't too shabby.

Who is the most overrated?

I guess it's Ray Felton, somehow. There are a decent number of players overseas I'd rather have.

Why do you enjoy reporting?

I like getting to the bottom of things.

I'm curious and a bit nosy (in a good way) by nature. In this field in particular, I'm incredibly passionate about sports, so to let people know what's going on with their team is rewarding. I like giving people an inside look that's normally sort of tough to find. Who's playing the post-game music? What World Cup team is Brendan Ryan screaming about? Who recently purchased a PhunkeeDuck?

Stuff like that. Sports should be fun.

ALLIE GOERTZ

🐦 @AllieGoertz

Allie is a musician and comic whose obsession with pop-culture
and *feelings* has born an album of nerdy love songs, a Rick and Morty
concept album, two popular TV-themed podcasts (Everything's Coming
Up Podcast and Fire Talk With Me) and a troubling Twitter addiction.
Since releasing her first crowd-sourced album in 2013, she's been touring
the country opening for and playing alongside her favorite comics and
musicians. She currently works in hazy Los Angeles as a social media
producer for @midnight.

What's interesting or uninteresting about Long Beach?

Long Beach is a particularly interesting place to grow up due
to its diverse background and versatility. I grew up in middle class
suburbia, my mom taught school in a lower income neighborhood
where most students were ESL, I went to a predominantly white
high school for three years, then a predominantly Hispanic high
school for my last, and the last place I lived was affectionately
dubbed "The Gay Ghetto."

There is something for everybody in Long Beach, at least for
a little while.

What do your parents do for a living?

My mom is nearing her retirement from teaching kindergarten, and my dad is a web graphic designer as well as a guitarist.

When did you first start playing the guitar?

My dad is an extremely talented guitarist and always encouraged me to play. I've been playing since I was 5 years old and have recently gotten more into it.

Can you talk about the origin story behind Cossbysweater? Why did you begin creating acoustic fan fiction?

Cossbysweater was my old moniker which I retired as soon as news broke out about Bill Cosby. At that point, I took the opportunity to publicly distance myself from his name.

In terms of my musical act, I released my first song "Comedians" three years ago on YouTube after playing it live for a number of weeks on Chatroulette. Surprised and inspired by the amount of attention it got, I decided to continue writing and publishing my music to YouTube. Eventually, I was approached by Adam Busch to make an album together. The release of "Cossbysweater" led to me being a part of the comedy scene in LA, performing my songs at various comedy shows.

How does performing a song on stage differ from performing jokes?

My music is comedic in many ways, but I would never describe it as straight up "comedy." That being said, I have found that my songs work in comedy venues because the audience is prepared to listen to the lyrics more intently than say, a music-only show. While I don't tell written material on stage, I have greatly enjoyed using banter and telling little stories in between songs as an additional means of comedy. I find myself talking more on more than when I started, and believe I will continue to head in this direction.

Some key differences between what I do and what stand-ups do are in the mechanics. I have guaranteed built-in applaud breaks as soon as my songs are done, and I always have the comfort of having a guitar on stage with me. I never have to worry about awkward pauses or silence. That said, I also don't get the liberty of working with the room. There's no bailing on a half-baked joke premise if my song doesn't seem to be clicking with the audience. There are advantages and disadvantages to both, but I think the key to either is to just enjoy what you're doing and trust that the audience will follow.

How did you get your start on @midnight? What tips would you give comics that want to work on a TV show?

I got my start on @midnight by publicly posting that I was looking for work. I had happened to know an executive producer for a new show starring Chris Hardwick that was doing test-runs at Meltdown and I decided to check it out. The EP, who had seen my online presence, suggested I apply for the job and I ended up getting it. My advice is to always ask for what you need. No one is going to know you are looking for work if you haven't told them, and in my experience, people want to help each other out. Let people help you.

Why do some jokes work on the internet and others don't?

I feel like I only recently got a handle on my joke-writing sense of humor. Thanks to reading tweets of people much MUCH funnier than I am every single day, I've gotten a better idea of what works and what doesn't. Twitter is an amazing tool because you really get to see whether or not people like your joke. Did it get likes? Did it get RT's? If not, there's a good chance you could have worded it better or that the premise won't read (well). Some people are naturally funny but will never be good at Twitter, and some people are the exact opposite; they're "Twitter funny" but not "IRL funny."

It's a very interesting thing and I love thinking about it.

What's on your horizon?

I just wrapped on my most recent project which was a Rick and Morty concept album entitled Sad Dance Songs. I am currently writing a pilot that I would love to shop around or get made (that's the dream, right?) and have plans of a Weezer cover album.

Who is the funniest person you know?

Paul B. Cummings.

Why are jokes funny?

They're not.

MIKE LAWRENCE

🐦 *@TheMikeLawrence*

Mike is a New York City based comedian from South Florida who has found success in both writing and stand up. He is a staff writer on the upcoming season of Inside Amy Schumer and was a writer on the 2015 MTV Movie Awards, the 2015 Webby Awards, and We Have Issues on E! Mike is a recurring guest on the Comedy Central's @midnight and his stand-up has been featured on Late Night with Seth Meyers, CONAN, Tottally Biased and John Oliver's New York Stand-Up Show.

What did you parents do for a living when you were a kid?

Mom was a comedian/chef and my dad worked in a hospital making sure it was up to code.

What's interesting or uninteresting about Hollywood (Florida)?

The first episode of Cops was filmed in my hometown

Why did you first want to start performing comedy? What was the first joke or bit you tried on stage?

I'd done poetry for years but was getting more and more laughs and it was just a natural direction. The first bit was about mixing whites and colors and being racist only at the laundromat. It's a very basic joke tons of other comics do but I certainly thought it was unique and funny at the time.

What advice would you give a comedian that's trying to get noticed?

Make sure it's unique, have many platforms and ideas, and enjoy what you do.

What was your first performance on TV?

My first TV performance was on John Oliver's New York Stand Up Show, which was on my 28th birthday. It was crazy but huge. Lots of pressure but it also felt like I had made it at a certain point.

What is the Nerd of Mouth origin story?

Me and Jake Young had fun talking comics and wanted other people to hear our dumb Batman conversations.

Do you prefer forming jokes on paper or on stage? Why?

Basic ideas on paper. I like taking them wherever I can and just trying things a hundred ways onstage.

What do you like or dislike about comedy in New York?

Love that you can make money and that the crowds are often demanding. Hate that there are some shows that charge money and don't pay comics and some of the indifferent audience members who are on their phone the whole time. That and a lot of people don't want to sit in the front row.

Who is the funniest person you know?

Everyone at Schumer blows me away. My buddies Dan St. Germain and Sean Patton are up there too.

What's the dumbest superhero name you can think of?

Cable. It doesn't even mean anything. A lot of X-Men names sound like someone looked at their kids 8th grade vocabulary sheet and picked their favorite words. "Rogue? That'll work!"

ALISON ZEIDMAN

@alisonlzeidman

Alison is a New York-based stand-up comedian and writer who got her start in Philly. Her humor writing has been featured in the New York Times, Time Out New York and Reductress. She's also known for her dedicated topical jokewriting online; a dumb, short-lived internet stunt; and her dark, personal stand-up material, delivered with a stage presence that has been described as "confidently anxious."

Where did you grow up?

I grew up in Moorestown, New Jersey, which is a small suburban town outside of Philadelphia. It was kind of a weird place to live, because about half of it is *very* wealthy, and the other half (my half) is not. Like, mansions and NFL players and teenagers driving BMWs on one half, and on my half…well, there's a McDonald's. (But it's one of the fancy McDonald'ses! Recently renovated to seem more European or whatever!)

There's also a lovely man-made lake (toxic cesspool) near my mom's house which is kind of nice to walk around and a frequent hot spot for divorcées who want somewhere to make out after they've had a forced meet-cute at a Starbucks. I really didn't feel like I fit in there growing up, but now when I go back to visit my mom I think, "Oh, this won't be such a terrible place to have to move back to when I have my inevitable breakdown." I'm just waiting for my own Silver Linings Playbook.

When did you realize you wanted to work in comedy?

Wait, work? You mean, you can do this as a *career*? Like, get *paid* for it consistently? Without having to have *another job* outside of it? Wow. Right now, I guess. Real answer: For sure around 2011, as soon as I started doing it in Philly. But I'd thought about it off and on since I first started watching stand-up specials and writing funny junk in middle school. I've been busting my ass to make it a career ever since, but it's definitely not the primary way I pay my bills — yet.

That being said, I feel like I've picked up a lot in my 9–5 life that's been useful in terms of marketing and promoting shows, being disciplined about my writing schedule, and just learning how to deal with people professionally in general. If you can balance both, I don't think having a steady day job is a bad thing or makes you less of an "artist."

That being said, if I could do it all over again, honestly I think I would just shoot straight to the top after my first open mic and let HBO give me a multi-million dollar advance to develop my own show. Hindsight, right?

What's the story behind Dark Spots at The Creek and Cave?

The short story is: My dad died, I started writing jokes about it, and I wanted a place where I'd never feel weird about doing that. I mean I'll do them in any room, but obviously not every crowd is coming to a comedy show because they want to hear about some stranger's hot take on her dead parent. They want to hear about some stranger's hot take on Tinder dating!

The slightly longer (but still not that long) story is: I was staying with my mom for the month after my dad died, and I was hanging out a little bit at Helium, the club in Philly, and doing some shows. That's when I first met Shane Torres (Comedy Bang Bang, CONAN), one of the guys I co-host and -produce *Dark*

Spots with. He had just moved to NYC from Portland, where they also have a Helium, and he was in Philly featuring. He had some jokes about his own dad dying, and we ended up talking that night and becoming really good friends. A month or two later, I had the idea for *Dark Spots*, and we started fine-tuning it together. For example, we knew we wanted the show to be dark, but not necessarily just cover traditionally dark subjects, like death. The monthly themes were Shane's idea.

We decided to bring on a third comic since Shane is on the road a lot, and the first person I thought of was Nate Fridson (Bridgetown Comedy Festival, AST Records). I ran into him when I first got back to New York and started doing my dead dad jokes, and he was really into them and encouraging, which meant a ton to me early on in doing those jokes, when I still wasn't sure whether or not it was something I should be writing about. (For lots of reasons. I've talked more about that ongoing uncertainty in a thing I barfed all over the internet on the train one night recently here.) Also, in the last six months four of Nate's family members have died. Four! So now he's *really* the perfect co-producer for the show.

I see comedy as a way to punch back, so to speak, at things that are terrifying or horrible or...just plain stupid. I love that our show gives comics a place to do that with some of their darkest experiences and the world's most fucked up events, and I really enjoy writing new bits and sketches to open the show with Shane and Nate every month. It's like having our own tiny little writers' room.

Can you walk me through your writing process? How do you prepare and execute long-form editorials?

Well, first I get an idea, and I get really excited about it. If I can't start on it right away, I'll write it down in a notebook, or in the Notes app on my phone, and hope that later on I'll remember what I meant by something like "realistic bathroom wall graffiti also remember to pick up birth control razors."

Then, before I sit down to write a new project, I have to…not procrastinate—I don't really do that—but just be anxious and nervous about whether or not I'll be able to write anything good. That'll haunt me until finally my schedule is clear, and I get the calendar alert on my phone for the time I planned to write whatever the thing is. That alert will be labeled as something really motivating, like "JUST FUCKING WRITE SOMETHING IDIOT." And then I start writing, and everything's fine, and I really enjoy it.

For stand-up and humor pieces like what I've done for the *New York Times*, for the most part I'll just go ahead and write and let myself have the fun of discovering ideas as they come out, and then edit later. For something like a sketch or pilot script though, I've learned the hard way that it's better to have a tight, detailed outline before you even get into the writing. It's painful, especially with the longer stuff, but pays off when you can just have fun and play in the dialogue because you did that work to figure out all the beats.

Why do you think it might be hard to meet new people? And to grow those connections?

Who says I have trouble meeting new people and connecting with them? Oh, everything I've ever written? OK, good point. I can only speak for myself, but I think for me it's probably hard because I no longer take any anxiety medications. I've decided I'm a high-functioning neurotic. Like it's bad, but not *that* bad, you know? Besides, the fact that I'm aware of it means I can just embrace it and be fun with it. Right? Oh geez, maybe I should go back to therapy.

Why do you think writers become writers?

So they can go to their high school reunions and say "I'm a writer now." And then find that no one's impressed. Even if *their* big life update was, "I substitute teach. And I smoke a *ton* of pot."

What do you enjoy most about comedy in New York?

You can do so much here, all the time. Actually, you don't have a choice—if you're not doing everything all the time, you're probably going to get a little lost. Or at least feel pretty bad about yourself. Luckily, I really like working, and I thrive on the pace of the New York scene, and the city in general.

I feel like being in this environment has made me work harder in ways I never even imagined, and it's made me a better comic and a better writer. I've also met a lot of the most amazing, funniest, best people I know here. It can be a tough place, but I wouldn't want to be anywhere else.

Who do you draw inspiration from as a comedian?

I guess I'll just list some of my favs? As far as the biggies go, it's Maria Bamford, Patton Oswalt, Tina Fey, Julia Louis Dreyfus, Michaela Watkins, Jon Stewart, Issa Rae… I could list a bunch of friends and peers, too, but I don't want to seem like I'm choosing favorites or accidentally leave anyone off who might take it personally.

Plus, some of my friends just are *not* funny. Like, *at all.* And I'd hate for them to find out here. Let's just let 'em wonder who I'm talking about instead! (I don't mean that. Everyone is the best.)

What makes a joke funny?

If I wrote it.

Wait, that sounds obnoxious. Sorry. Uhh…how about, "If it gets mad Facebook likes."

JANINE BRITO

🐦 *@janinebrito*

Janine is a stand-up comic, and was a writer and on-air correspondent on the FX series Totally Biased with W. Kamau Bell produced by Chris Rock. She's also half Cuban, half Icelandic, and aaaall lesbian. Janine started doing standup comedy in St. Louis and has performed at clubs and theaters throughout the US and Hong Kong. She is the winner of the 2009 SF Women's Comedy Competition, and recipient of Rooftop Comedy's 2010 Silver Nail Award.

Why do you think men catcall women?

Because some men are under the delusion that a woman needs to know about their attraction. But she doesn't need to know that, she's just trying to be a person in the world and she doesn't need to be made to feel like an object. She's not going to be flattered, she's going to feel violated and gross.

Listen, I GET seeing a beautiful woman and thinking "boi-oioioioioiiiiing!" trust me. And look at me, LOOK AT ME. I'm hot, yet I know better than to say a goddamn thing, so shut your 4-on-your-best-day-lookin' ass up.

Do you find that your culture (half-Cuban and half-Icelandic) influences your comedy?

Yes, I'm from Miami and didn't start learning how to speak English until kindergarten so a lot of my experience stems from looking in on the outside. But my mom's side being white and frequent visits to Alabama help me understand how to get middle America to hear me. Folksy whiteness is the spoon full of sugar that helps the other shit go down.

What do you enjoy most about comedy festivals?

Eating a million times more than I should, after hours dance parties, hanging out with people I love in a new setting, and meeting new people who are bomb.

What do you dislike most?

That neck craning thing some comics do to see if there's a bigger name in the room than you. Chill and be a person for a minute, bruh.

What makes for a good writers room?

Different, funny voices. Look, I love Harvard white boys but there are only so many smirk jokes I can take. Give me something that's going to make me scream with laughter. Give me some Leslie Jones shit. Give me some Dwayne Kennedy shit. Give me some Aparna Nancherla shit.

Who are some of your comedic influences?

Maria, I saw her first Comedy Central Presents when I was in high school and was instantly obsessed. My dad, my comedy friends, and perfectly-timed farts.

Why do you think comedians become comedians?

Oh absolutely because we're broken. I was a chubby closeted-case from a home of divorce who was essentially raised by a paranoid schizophrenic, this wasn't going to end up in marketing.

Do you think we'll ever have an openly-gay president?

Yes, because gays get shit done while looking beautiful. Plus, we're not limited to one place or family, we pop up everywhere. So eventually everyone will have a gay friend or family member they love and that personal love goes a long way in dismantling homophobia.

What makes a joke funny?

A premise that elicits that feeling of 'I think this all the time!'

...and grows into 'I would have never thought of this genius thing but it makes perfect sense now that I have heard it, this person is the Einstein of human experience!'

DAN WILBUR

🐦 *@DanWilbur*

Dan has been doing stand-up for over ten years. In that time, he's also written for College Humor, McSweeney's, The Onion News Network on IFC, Someecards, Reader's Digest, and a couple web series you've never heard of that paid him with checks that said, verbatim: "Cheese Jokes." He also wrote a humor book for Penguin in 2012 called How Not to Read: Harnessing the Power of a Literature-Free Life. Dan co-hosts a weekly stand-up show at UCB East Village called Lasers in the Jungle every Thursday night at 7:30 PM.

Do you think there's a misconception about people from the Midwest?

No. We're sweet. We're people-pleasing and nice, and not in a backhanded "bless his heart" Southern way that's about manners. In a genuinely nice, "I'm here to make sure everyone feels comfortable and has a good time" kind of way. The problem is: not everyone likes nice people.

The misconception, at least for Cleveland, is that there's nothing to do in the Midwest. I heard a comic do a bit about how teens did more drugs in the Midwest than in NYC because all you could do in the Midwest was take acid and drive around, whereas in New York there's constant entertainment. The second I had a car in Cleveland though, I went to an indie movie theater called Cedar Lee twice a week, I was a regular at a coffee shop where filmmakers and writers hung out, I started theater at six, improv at

---

146

12, I was a drummer, touring Broadway shows came to us, the Indians were in the World Series every other year in the '90s, the Browns came back right when I started playing football in high school, I saw LeBron play live at least 30 times (and the tickets were $15). I mean… I also smoked pot and drove my car around. There's time for all of that. What I'm trying to say is: you can't be bored in Cleveland. That's a misconception.

You studied creative writing at Bard. Are there tricks you picked up in college that you still use today?

Yes! Sometimes you don't have the idea until it's coming out of your mouth (or on paper). The best feeling in the world as a comic is to have a thought on the way to a show, never even put it on paper, say it out loud, and get a laugh. I learned that writing on stage is the same as the collaborative process of talking with other students in class about an idea. Being put on the spot in front of a room of your peers who are by all accounts more intelligent than you are, that's when you are really forced to get to the point as quickly as possible, even when you're not sure what you're trying to say. It sounds like I bullshitted a lot in college… I did.

Bad bullshit is speaking like you're an authority even when you know you're not, but good bullshit is knowing you're an idiot, admitting it, and still meandering until you find a nugget of truth. Aha! As I write this, I realize I'm regurgitating Socrates, the smartest man on Earth because he knows that which he does not know. Even though he was aware of his ignorance, it didn't stop him from talking. That's a comic in a nutshell.

Congratulations on your new book—Never Flirt with Puppy Killers and Other Better Book Titles. How did you originally come up with the idea for the series?

The blog came out of years of reading with the intention of writing a novel, but having a disdain for pretension. I think that's a Bard thing. You're given more reading per semester than anyone possibly could finish, then you're supposed to synthesize all that information in a paper that plainly states your own ideas about a book. What else can you do except say, "the message of this book has nothing to do with its vague, pretentious title! It's all about sex!"

The real lightbulb moment was about a year after college. I was playing Assassin's Creed with a friend, and at the end of the game you strangle a pope, and I said to my friend "Strangle the Pope" would have been a better title for this game.

What advice would you give someone trying to get his or her book published?

The same advice I'd give comics: keep doing it, find your voice, make sure you actually enjoy it. Sounds really vague and unhelpful, but there's a reason people say it: it works. It's gratifying to be validated by some already formed entity in publishing or entertainment, but anyone who does it for a while knows it's more gratifying to put your own work out there. And if something you do on your own really takes off, people in your industry will take note. So keep doing the work you enjoy, find a community that supports it, get advice, help your friends, ask your friends for help, keep doing it.

I think if I could do it over in publishing specifically, I would have spent some years as an editor first. The people I know who enjoy the publishing world, who start at entry-level jobs assisting editors seem to like it and have a better vision of what gets published and have a better idea of what they like in a book and what they don't like. You also have the privilege of seeing a book before it's perfect. It's always easier to see flaws in someone else's writing, and if you can get an eye for that when you're young, it will be easier to self-edit without getting discouraged. No one is good at writing! It takes 16 drafts before you can even show it to someone.

Do you have a different writing process for doing stand-up vs. writing a book?

This book in particular is exactly like stand-up. It's jokes that I wrote over years and years all together in one spot. You see someone do five minutes on Late Night, it's not five minutes of work propelling them into being a working comic, it's years of writing jokes and perfecting them, presented in five minutes. That's how I feel about this book. It's a decade of thinking about books, six years of writing one idea, presented to readers as something they can read very quickly.

As far as writing, in general, versus stand-up? You should show more people your drafts and get direct feedback. Stand-up's easier in a way because you do it all the time and you get immediate feedback. If you do a joke six times in two days, you at least know if the premise has legs. A novel or a short story you might sit on for months before you have the guts to show it to someone. I'd say if you have an idea for a novel, write down some beats, and get coffee with some trusted friends, and see if their eyes glaze over as you talk it out.

Your show at UCB East has had a ton of great comedians on as guests. What works best about the space there?

Anya Garrett (my girlfriend) is responsible for those lineups, and I think people come to see a good comedy show rather than any one person, and that's what makes it good. We're putting on the show we'd pay money to see. I think we have a lot of repeat audience members because the show is steady (it runs exactly 70 minutes every week, so there's no time to be bored). I love theme shows like See You In Hell and Punderdome! I wish I could come up with a funny concept show, but until then, consistent time/place/great comics, people will come out.

Why do you think comedians become comedians?

I think every comic loves the form and has a chip on his or her shoulder. I don't mean "enjoying a stand-up special once a year." I mean loving it. Wanting to fill most of your time thinking about it if not actually listening to it. Loving stand-up means you have a deep, dark void in your soul where joy should be. Believing you could do it means you're out to prove something. You need both. A big enough ego to want people to pay attention to you, but not enough self-esteem to go into politics. That's a comedian.

What makes a joke funny?

I have no idea.

I read Freud in college. It didn't help. The funniest stand-up takes something everyone cares about, and destroys it... or takes something no one cares about and elevates it to the level of idolatry. You could also time a fart really well. That's always funny.

WILL MILES

🐦 *@MrWillMiles*

Will is a New York based stand-up comedian. In 2015, Miles was featured on truTV's Friends Of The People, Bravo's Guide To…, Fusion TV's Come Here and Say That and MTV's Middle of the Night Show. Miles has also been featured in The New York Times, The New Yorker, Buzzfeed and The Huffington Post. Will can be seen on season two of The Chris Gethard Show, where he is also a writer.

Where did you grow up?

I grew up in Chicago, Illinois on the North Side.

What's interesting or uninteresting about the North Side?

I grew up in Boys Town, a predominantly gay neighborhood, which is right next to Wrigley Field, where the Chicago Cubs play, and most known for having a lot of frat dudes around. My elementary school was between my neighborhood and the Cabrini Green Housing Projects, one of the most well-known housing projects in the country before it was torn down.

Growing up around all of these extreme differences made it hard to fit into an exact social group, but it also made me a chameleon in terms of my friendships in life.

What did your parents do for a living when you were a kid?

My dad was a lawyer, politician, and is currently an investment banker. My mom worked in politics, was a nurse, and now works at an elementary school in the office. When I stop by her office, it appears the entire school relies on her in some way.

What was the first bit or joke you performed on stage?

The first bit I performed on stage was a bit about how one time I was high before bed with the Food Network on, and I dreamed about having a penis so large I could have sex with Rachael Ray in one room while being in the other room watching TV. It went over well at first, but I'm so happy it started bombing early on, so I had to stop doing it.

When and where did you become a regular?

The first places I became a regular were Town Hall Pub and Zanies. Town Hall Pub was a bar that used to have big punk and house-hip-hop parties with groups like Flosstradamus and Matt and Kim, and then turned into a comedy venue where I was a regular along with comedians like Jena Friedman, Beth Stelling, Hannibal Buress, and many more.

One of my best friends, Julia, was the bartender during both the parties and the comedy shows. Zanies Comedy Club in Old Town is one of the oldest comedy clubs in Chicago. It's my home club and Bert Haas is one of my favorite people in the world.

The Knitting Factory also seems to be a great space for comedy. How did your relationship with them begin?

It originally began as a show hosted by Hannibal Buress, who I've known since before I was a stand-up comedian. He built up the room for about five years and then got really busy so he handed it off to me, Clark Jones, and Kenny DeForest. We had all come and done it when he hosted throughout the years, and we moved here when he was ready to hand it off.

I first did the show in about the second or third month it existed, so it was essential in my comedic growth over the last five years, as well. It's always been a great space and I love hosting with two of my best friends every week. We owe Hannibal a bunch for giving the show to us.

What do you like or dislike about comedy in New York?

I love the access to stage time. There are so many chances to work on your act in any given night. Even when network people or agents come to shows, they come because they are actually enjoying the process of stand-up comedy. They even stay to watch the whole show. The only thing I dislike is the NYC open mic. I came from Chicago, where real people come to see open mics and you can get good responses from actual audience. In NYC, open mics are all comics, so it's a little harder to judge what will work on a club or showcase stage.

Do you prefer forming jokes on paper or on stage?

I prefer building a skeleton offstage on paper but I have to work it out onstage to understand the punches and lock down the structure of what I'm trying to say. When I throw a new joke in the middle of a set, I understand my voice better and figure out the right word economy I need to make the joke funny.

I read once that Louis CK starts with his closer when he's developing an act, so I've been doing that. It really helps me write in my best comedic voice.

Any thoughts on the Drake-Meek Mill battle?

I love rap. I grew up listening to Pharcyde, NWA, Tribe Called Quest, etc., and my daily life is influenced by having grown up on that music. Currently, Drake has been completely destroying Meek Mill and will be the reason Meek Mill's album sales drop from now on. I feel bad for how horribly he is treating Meek Mill, but I'd be lying if I didn't say I enjoyed watching it from afar. I mean, Drake got Will Smith and Kanye West to join in on the ridicule. That's downright mean.

What are your three favorite romantic comedies and why?

My favorite rom com is Forgetting Sarah Marshall. I think it is a really great story about how when you try to make love happen, it's probably the wrong choice, but when it just happens, you know in your heart that you've made the right choice. Every cameo is excellent and it's a realistic journey to the "right one." This is why I also love "The Wedding Planner." Beyond the fact that I think Matthew McConaughey is one of the best actors around, the Wedding Planner is a great story of how he was with the wrong woman but ended up falling in love with his soul mate completely on accident. When you find your soulmate, it's undeniable, and I think that really comes through in this story.

My other favorite is The Wood. While it's mostly a coming of age tale, the fact that Omar Epps' character had to go through his entire life journey before he realized he has been in love with the same girl since the day he first laid eyes on her in 7th grade is a really beautiful love story. The supporting cast from the adults to the children really give their best performances, and the movie has always been one of my favorites.

Who is the funniest person you know?

My grandfather has never cared about saying the right thing, and that always makes me laugh. He is proof that if your intent is not to hurt someone, your words can still be very funny. He has a good heart, so I know he would never hurt anyone, but he also doesn't watch what he says and I laugh hard whenever he says things that could be taken as politically incorrect.

Why are jokes funny?

They are thoughts we wish we could have all the time.

If everything could be looked at through a humorous take, life wouldn't be so hard. Most comedians have at least a little bit of anxiety, narcissism, or depression, so looking at the humorous side of things is the way we cope internally and help others externally.

KENNY DeFOREST

@KennyDeForest

Kenny is a Brooklyn-based comic known best as a producer and co-host of Comedy at the Knitting Factory, widely considered to be one of New York's best independently run comedy shows. He has also appeared on TruTV's Friends of the People and was a writer for Season 1 of MTV's Bugging Out.

What's your name and where did you grow up?

My name is Kenny DeForest and I grew up in Springfield, MO. Springfield is interesting because it's a rapidly growing city that has a major college in it, but it's also in the Bible Belt. So we have a unique blend of a burgeoning art scene, great food culture, and science and innovation, but we also have mega-churches that send voters in out droves. Unless I missed the reversal, it's technically legal to discriminate against LGBT folks in Springfield, MO and we also voted for the "legitimate rape" guy Todd Aiken?

What did your parents do for a living when you were a kid?

My dad runs a farm supply business with my uncle that my grandfather started. They now have three locations across south Missouri.

What was the first bit or joke you performed on stage?

It was a joke about STDs and how a woman once responded "Like, right now?" to the question "Do you have anything I should know about?" I actually ad-libbed the punch-line my first time on stage which was "Yeah — obviously I'm asking about right now. I already know what you're gonna have tomorrow..."

I would say the Chicago Laugh Factory is where I took the biggest stride. It opened in 2012, I believe, and suddenly there was this 300-seat club that mostly booked local comics. I was lucky to get in there early on. Consistently having 20 minute sets in that environment was so important to my development.

How did you start producing and hosting at The Knitting Factory and what kind of show do you put on?

We (myself, Clark jones, Will Miles along with booker/producer Luisa Diez) took over for Hannibal Buress once Hannibal got too busy to run the show. Hannibal started the show years ago and grew it in to a very popular, well-attended show. I would say it's the best show in New York, but I'm biased.

We've been running it for almost a year now and I like to think we've carried on the tradition quite well. We just try to put on the best show possible and showcase our favorite comics. We host the show together and our chemistry is great after years of friendship. I definitely think seeing three guys riffing about the news of the week and making fun of each other is a fun look for the audience.

Do you prefer building jokes on paper or on stage?

On stage for sure. I write much better when there's an audience in front me. I like having the added pressure to find the funny. That said, I write things on paper to get them out of my head and written down.

What do you like or dislike about comedy in New York?

New York City is the center of the comedy universe. The best comedians on earth are on New York; if not permanently, they at least come to New York regularly.

There's nowhere else on earth you can see such a high level of stand-up comedy on a nightly basis.

Comedians In Public is such a crazy, fun idea. How did that come about? What has the response been?

Matt Ott approached me about doing it and told me who had already agreed to do it. I've got a real Marty McFly "nobody calls me chicken" complex. I can't back down from a challenge. This is also why I've performed stand-up comedy naked.

Why do some jokes work on the internet and others don't?

Jokes online lack tone and context. It's hard to be nuanced in writing. Jokes that work online tend to be simple. Usually the tweets I almost don't tweet because of how embarrassingly dumb they are the ones that get the most love.

Who is the funniest person you know?

My grandpa Joe Kenny is the funniest person I've ever known. Great story teller. Classic Irish barroom story teller. As he got older, he would repeat stories all the time, but we never stopped him because they were so good every time.

Why are jokes funny?

Because conscious existence is kind of a cruel joke.

None of us know why we're here. We're dumb animals that think we're smart so we pretend we know why we're here and act accordingly with way too much confidence. This combination of utter confusion and absolute certainty surrounding our own existence is inherently funny. That and because online dating is weird.

CYRUS McQUEEN

🐦 *@CyrusMMcQueen*

Cyrus is a comedian and actor. He was named One of the Sexiest Men in New York by the New York Post. He can be seen in the film Obvious Child and was a semifinalist on Last Comic Standing.

Where did you grow up?

I grew up in Roxbury, a town in the inner city of Boston. One interesting thing about Roxbury is that it's where Martin Luther King stayed while getting his Masters from Boston University. It's also where Malcolm X came of age.

Where's the first place you performed stand up?

I first performed stand up at New York Comedy Club at an open mic in 2009. I performed stand up because friends and family had been pushing me to do it for years. At the time I'd taken so many classes and spent so much money at UCB, but still couldn't get on one of their house teams, so I said to hell with improv, let me finally try this.

I'd already gotten a ton of radio work doing impressions of Obama, Sam Jackson, etc. so my first joke ever was an impression of Obama hiding cigarettes around the White House. But I'd always been a class clown, all the way up through drama school. I got kicked off the school bus, I got detention, all for making the other kids laugh. (And possibly because I *was* disrupting class.)

How did you get on Last Comic Standing?

I ended up on Last Comic Standing because I was able to finagle an audition for it. I should mention, I worked as the door guy at a comedy club for 12 years. After I started comedy, they still wouldn't give me stage time, so I essentially begged them to at least give me an audition for the show.

What led to landing your role in Obvious Child?

I got the role in Obvious Child randomly. I don't have representation, but have managed to capitalize on the few opportunities I have been given. A casting director was in the audience at one of my shows.

She called me in for another movie which I booked, but at the last minute they gave the role to someone with a bigger name, but she promised to bring me in again, and that second audition was for Obvious Child, which I was blessed to have gotten.

New York vs. Los Angeles?

The only comedy I've done in L.A. was on Last Comic, so that's not necessarily the best barometer of the L.A. scene. I love New York cause you can hustle here. Go up several times a day. What I dislike about both scenes is, if you're on the outside looking in, it's hard to make a name for yourself. On both coasts there are far more comedians than there are spots to perform, so that can be daunting.

But I mostly dislike how young, powerful, exciting comedians aren't given the club work they should because of politics. Having worked in a comedy club for over a decade, I can tell you, at open mics/bar shows in NYC, you'll see more special talent and palpable energy than you will at a comedy club.

What makes something funny?

The natural formula of set-up and punch.

But also, and perhaps more profoundly, what makes a joke funny is when a person recognizes a truth. A truth about the world, or a truth about themselves. As comedians we're merely exploring life's truths and hypocrisies. As a comedian I'm basically holding a mirror up to the audience as well as myself.

JOE LIST

🐦 *@JoeListComedy*

Joe is a comedian and has a weekly podcast called 'Tuesdays with Stories'. He has appeared on Last Week Tonight, Last Comic Standing, Conan and the Late Show with David Letterman.

Where did you grow up?

I grew up in Whitman, Massachusetts.

What's interesting or uninteresting about Whitman?

What's interesting about the place I grew up is that it claims to be where the chocolate chip cookie was invented.

What was the first bit or joke you performed on stage?

The first jokes I ever told on stage were: "I went to that bar 'Cheers' …nobody knew my name." and "I went to Boston Celtics game…lot of empty seats for a team called the 'Sell-Tix.'"

(I was 18)

When and where did you become a regular?

I became a regular at the Comedy Connection in Boston around 2002. It's no longer there and I miss it. From late 2002 until it closed in, I think 2008, I was there all the time.

I loved it dearly and still miss it.

What do you like or dislike about comedy in New York?

What I love about the comedy scene in New York is that there are so many places to perform. There's a lot of good clubs and a couple of really great ones. There's a great alt scene, a lot of good bar shows, a ton of open mic and just a lot of really creative and fun places to perform.

I find it to be a really supportive scene. There's a lot of great comics, I love it.

Can you walk me through the day you performed on The Late Show with David Letterman?

The day I did Letterman, I woke up and went to the gym, I did a quick workout and then took a steam. Then I went to downtown Manhattan and met up with my friend (name drop) Colin Quinn. We had lunch together. Then I took the subway to Penn Station and met up with my parents who had taken the train down from Boston. They got a hotel a few blocks from the Ed Sullivan Theater. We checked into the hotel, then we ate Chipotle. My friend Jason Kanter and his dad Fred then joined us (they brought my suit). A little later my girlfriend Sarah Tollemache joined us. We hung around the hotel for a while, then we all walked together to the theater. At the theater I met up with my pals (more name dropping) Gary Gulman and Nick DiPaolo.

My parents, Fred and Jason went in and sat in the audience. Sarah, Gary, Nick and my then manager Maureen Taran and I all went up to the dressing room and just sort of hung around for a while. It was very low key and enjoyable. Around 10 minutes before I went on, I took the elevator down to the stage level and waited there for a few minutes. Then when it was time I took the stage, blacked out, came to, shook hands with Dave and then came back to the green room.

When I got there I hugged Gary and Nick and Maureen and Sarah. After the show I met back up with my parents and friends. We took some pictures on stage and at Dave's desk. Then we went and got pizza at Lombardi's downtown. Then ended the night at the Comedy Cellar. Probably the best day of my life.

How did The Ultimate Worrier series start?

The Ultimate Worrier started as a tweet. I think I tweeted something like "If I were a wrestler, I would be the 'Ultimate Worrier'. And then I just thought that that would be a really funny character. A guy who dresses like the Ultimate Warrior but instead just worries about everything. There honestly wasn't a ton of thought put into it other than that. I had my friend Dan Hirshon help me. He shot it and edited it for me and did a great job. There was no real script or anything, I just talked about some of the things I worry about myself and exaggerated it a bit, and added some other ridiculous things that I don't actually worry about but thought would be funny if someone did worry about them. That was pretty much it.

Then I got a lot of positive feedback so I did a second series where The Ultimate Worrier interviewed people. Instead of asking them questions about their lives, I asked them about what they worry about and if they worried about things that I worried about. The whole thing was completely absurd, but people seem to really enjoy it.

What's the dumbest superhero name you can think of?

The dumbest superhero name I can think of is "Dumbman."

REGINAL THOMAS

🐦 *@ReginalThomas*

Reginal has been in the New York comedy scene for two full years. He's a regular at the New York Comedy Club where he headlines and Broadway Comedy Club. Aside from that he writes a comedy segment for the In The Mix With Shoom podcast found on Soundcloud.

Where did you grow up?

I grew up in Brooklyn; Home of the Brave.

How often do people call you Reginald?

All the time, people call me Reginald. My name is Reginal, with no D, so when it's time to correct them I usually say, "Look I got plenty of D just not in my name." But that doesn't bug me as much as its bugs me when people call me Reggie.

I hate that name! I prefer Reg.

What's interesting or uninteresting about Kensington?

I grew up in Kensington Village in Brooklyn and the whole area is basically Orthodox Jews and old immigrant Russians still bringing family members over from their old country. So I never really lived in a hood but hood things would happen like when a group of Muslim kids would walk through the neighborhood a brawl was bound to happen at least once or twice a year.

There is also this kind of 'Jewish neighborhood watch' that exists in my hood, so if you can picture little Jewish men hopping out of minivans with police lights on them trying to pull off a citizen's arrest on people; it's comical to me.

What did your parents do for a living when you were a kid?

By trade my father was a welder and my mom was a home help aid up until '97 then she was just a house mom raising me and my brother while my pops worked. But on the side my father was a great artist. I grew up with art in my life; my father made these beautiful oil paintings in the living room and would play Haitian music until the late hours of the night, so I got to see him create these great pieces and I think I've carried that with me in life.

What was the first bit or joke you performed on stage?

The first joke I performed on stage was about going on interviews for a job you don't even want and just the aggravating things they say to you on a job interview like: "We are more like a family here at the Gap so tell me why do you want to join this family?" And I'm like "Man, I don't even like my own family what the hell made you think I was in the market for a new one. I'm here 'cause I need a job!"

Adventures Behind the Blue Wall is a fantastic short. What was your inspiration behind the piece? How did you direct the shoot?

Thank you I'm happy you feel that way about it. My inspiration for the sketch was the Walter Scott video where the cop shot the guy eight times in the back and then dropped a Taser next to him to help prove a lie that Scott tried to grab his gun and put himself in the situation. Also I was inspired by black cops and how hush hush they always seem to be. In the eyes of the black community black cops come off as a total WTF sometimes. Once in a blue moon one of them speaks up but that's few and far between. Their relationship with black people might be just as damaged as regular white cops, if not more. But I have family who are cops and I know plenty of black cops and they're all great men and women who really service the community; but when it comes time to talk about the issues they side with the cops. And that's cool, I understand that part, but they just don't understand where the other black people are coming from. Talk can't just lead to one big argument about something we weren't even talking about in the first place.

So part of it was just finally giving a voice to black cops in a way. Finally, I just think it's crazy how easy is it to actually become a cop. There's nothing to it and I just wanted to shine a light on the fact that just about anyone can be put in such a powerful position. Wale is a great director and he worked the camera while I focused on the writing and making sure we delivered the lines the way I wanted.

How did Sole Comedy Show get started?

The Sole Comedy Show just premiered for the first time this past weekend so kudos on your research! Sole came about because I was presented with an opportunity to produce a new show at the New York Comedy Club. The previous shows I did were somewhat of a flop so I had to find a concept that I liked and was true to me — that was my love for kicks and looking fly.

I used to be a personality for a popular sneaker site a few years ago so I still have relationships in the sneakerhead world and there are plenty of comics who are sneakerheads. I decided I would produce a show where I bring the funniest comic sneakerheads together for one show and it was amazing. Then I hit up Flight Club, this great sneaker store in NYC, and they gave me some accessories in the shape of dope sneakers to give out at the show. I had some heavy hitters on there: Monroe Martin, Jordan Rock, Vladimir Caamano to name a few. It was a great show and I'm looking forward to producing another soon.

Do you prefer building jokes on paper or on stage? And why?

I prefer building jokes on paper because I'm constantly thinking I have something to prove or I just don't like looking unprepared. So I always write my jokes and go over them in my head and sometimes that way I will pick up a new tag or something. In my mind the audience always has to see me at my best so I don't do a new joke until I'm comfortable with where it's at before I present it to a crowd.

What do you like or dislike about comedy in New York?

I couldn't tell you that there was something I didn't like about the scene. One thing is for sure there are a lot of crazy people in the comedy scene but aside from that I like it. New York's full of young, talented comics who are constantly coming up with new jokes. I love to see people doing dope things in comedy; not the same mundane shit.

Who is the funniest person you know?

I know too many funny people to narrow it down to one so I will just say me.

What's on your horizon?

I'm producing more shows, Adventures Behind the Blue Wall is getting screened at a couple comedy shows in the next few weeks, Productively Stoned is still running strong and just continue to work in comedy. More shows finally get on the road.

Why are jokes funny?

Cause they make us look at real life and see all the exceptions.

Everyday people are told you can't do this until you see someone do it and jokes allow you to laugh at whatever it was that made you think otherwise.

SHANE MAUSS

🐦 *@shanecomedy*

Originally from Wisconsin, Shane caught his first break when he was awarded Best Stand-Up at The HBO US Comedy Arts Festival. This led to his TV debut and first of five appearances on Conan. Since that time, he's been on Jimmy Kimmel, Showtime, has had a Comedy Central Presents, a Netflix special 'Mating Season', and most recently released album inspired by breaking both of his feet in a hiking mishap called 'My Big Break' which spent time at #1 on the comedy iTunes charts.

Do Mausses secretly hate Mosses? What's the etymology behind your last name?

I'm told my ancestors were Jewish and went by the name "Mosche" (Hebrew word for 'Moses') in 17th century Switzerland. They changed it to Mauss (pronounced 'mose' in French) when they learned Jews couldn't own the land in France that the king was giving away. I'm German (and Irish now, so I can't make jokes about how stereotypically Jewish that move is.)

I never cared for my name and almost changed in to Moss at the start of my comedy career but never got around to it. I'm jealous of the Mosses. They make everyone's life easier.

You caught your first break at the HBO US Arts Festival. Can you walk me through what that day was like?

I seemed to be having really standout performances during the festival. I was very drunk the whole time, having fun, and making new friends. I wasn't taking it terribly seriously but it was weird because people kept on walking up to me in the streets and raving about how funny I was. It felt like I was a celebrity all of the sudden.

On the day of the awards, people running the festival kept on making sure that I would be there so I figured something was up. After I won, I had my pick of managers and agents. One of the Conan bookers was there and had me on shortly after. It was life changing.

What advice would you give a comedian that's making his or her first appearance on TV?

It's a different environment than performing in a club. It's not usually not nearly as intimate if it is late night. There is a whole camera crew between you and the audience. And many audience members are looking at you, they are watching the monitors, or the camera crew, or the hosts reaction. It's strange to look up and see people who are watching you but not looking at you.

And don't forget that people didn't show up there for a stand-up comedy show. They showed up to see how a taping of their favorite host works and maybe see some big celebrities. It's important to have your timing down the way you want it ahead of time and don't let the audience effect it negatively.

How did Here We Are first develop?

I've actually recorded over 80 episodes at this point. I've always been interested in science and reading about it here and there. Years ago I was in a new relationship and had just gotten out of a bad one so I was writing a lot of relationship material. I was also smoking more weed than normal and therefore watching a lot more Animal Planet. So I was writing a lot of animal jokes as well. The two started coming together and I started writing about and researching mating behavior.

Studying mating behavior led to an obsession with evolutionary psychology/biology—which led to branching out into more and more life sciences. I was working on putting a few ideas for projects together and reached out to some scientists for help. I became friends with some scientists and enjoyed our conversations so much that I thought it would make for a great podcast. It's been a really fun project. I learn a lot.

Why do you like talking about science so much?

I've always been a big thinker and a day dreamer. I like learning about big ideas and have questions about what I learn. Ideally I would just have the right person to call anytime that I have a question. Maybe that will happen eventually. Maybe that will be another project down the line or maybe something I eventually do as bonus episodes once I have a big enough network of people.

What do you like and/or dislike about comedy in Los Angeles?

I don't like that the clubs act like it is your privilege to spend your whole evening driving to and waiting around to do a short set to a mediocre audience. Appreciation should be a two-way street. That's one of the many reasons that I like all of the indie shows in town. Some of them like Meltdown are just so much better than any club show you will ever do.

What's the craziest thing you've seen on the road?

I tell a very long story about shows on the border of Mexico on my second appearance of Pete Holmes' You Made It Weird podcast that lots of people seemed to really enjoy. It's a very long story.

In five words or less, describe your comedy writing technique

Free-write, research, add, edit, test.

What makes a joke funny?

Humor is surprisingly complicated.

I've had three podcasts on this topic and I still can't tell you everything about it. There is a theory of psychologist Peter McGraw's that a joke needs to be just the right parts benign and a violation. Surprise is usually important. So is delivery. Also what makes people laugh and what is funny aren't always the same thing. This is an endless conversation. Listen to my podcasts about it for more.

APRIL BRUCKER

🐦 *@aprilbrucker*

April just wants a dude who can put up with 16 puppet children, a closet full of costumes, boxes of books and comics and her love for non-fiction history documentaries and pretzels. If you can deal with those things, you are Mr. Okay. Seeking Mr. Okay has given April a wealth of material for her stand-up performances at comedy clubs nationwide, plus has resulted in numerous television appearances, including "Cash Cab," CBS Sports Now, Entertainment Tonight, Inside Edition, Last Comic Standing, Layover With Anthony Bourdain, My Strange Addiction, No Reservations, Rachael Ray and The Today Show.

Where did you grow up?

I grew up in Bethel Park, PA, right outside of Pittsburgh. It's a suburb.

What's interesting or uninteresting about Bethel Park?

Interesting: It is where the Whiskey Rebellion took place. A Post-Revolutionary War skirmish, the Whiskey Rebellion occurred when the farmers revolted over The Whiskey Tax. The riot was squashed by federal troops. Also, there is a public access station in the town where I spent most of my teen years filming programs. Also, Andy Warhol is buried above the Washington Junction Trolley Stop in St. Anne's Cemetery.

Uninteresting: It's a suburb. It closes down relatively early, and if you want to go dancing that is not the place.

What did your parents do for a living when you were a kid?

My parents were both educators. My dad was a lawyer and a college professor, and my mom was an exercise physiologist and group fitness instructor who worked with all age groups. They were big on us being readers. The Encyclopedia Collection was my jam, and we weren't allowed television on school nights.

Only when I was 13 did my family finally get cable.

What was the first bit or joke you performed on stage?

The first bit I performed onstage was with a Groucho Marx figure (puppet) and it was a Christmas routine where Groucho sang "Lydia the Tattooed Lady" from Night at the Circus.

How were you first introduced to puppetry? What lessons have you learned along the way?

I was first introduced to puppetry/ventriloquism when I was 13-years-old. My brother had embarked on a career as a high school football player, and my father wanted to see the local games. In order to get one channel, you have to get 100. So thus we were forced to get cable. It opened up the world for this overweight, shy, awkward, teen who had braces with rubber bands and cystic acne. Anyway, my family was watching an Edgar Bergen TV Special and I was the only one in the house who could talk like a ventriloquist. It was due to my great-grandmother's Irish smile. That Christmas, my mom put a Groucho Marx ventriloquist figure under the tree.

What I enjoy most about ventriloquism is the ability to create a new character giving it a voice, personality and backstory. It's almost like I am a supreme being breathing life into her creation. Plus, they say whatever I want them to, whenever I want them to.

The lesson I have learned along the way is always to have fun and to keep learning. As a result, I have also become a student, and to some extent, mastered hand and rod as well as Balinese Shadow Puppetry.

You used to work for "Broadway Singing Telegrams" under "Bruce Myles Beaureguard." Is that what it sounds like? Can you talk about your time there?

Yes, I did and still do. Broadway Singing Telegrams and Bruce Myles Beaureguard are the fictional handles for Big Apple Singing Telegrams and Jon Shipley. Big Apple is an eccentric, talented, and diverse family. Jon is sort of the shepherd of our flock. My co-workers never cease to amaze me with their talent as well as their dedication. They are remarkable actors, musical theatre performers, impersonators, comedians, and vocalists. You have even seen a few on Broadway and national television. I have performed "Happy Birthday," "I'm Sorry," "Congratulations" and even proposed to a few people. I have been to offices, backyards, shipyards, hospitals, construction sites, Trump Towers and even broke into The Bloomberg Building.

I have dressed as a pink gorilla, chicken, cow, hot dog, pickle, M&M, Hershey Kiss, Birthday Cake Show Girl, pizza, female cop, naughty nurse, French Maid, Lady Gaga, Marilyn Monroe, Miley Cyrus, Madonna, Mae West, Taylor Swift, Suzanne Summers, and Paris Hilton just to name a few. I have also appeared as Billie Holiday via telephone.

Additionally, I have delivered to Betsey Johnson, the CEO of the NHL, execs at MTV, well-respected cancer researchers, The Saudi Royal Family and the Jordanian Royal Family. I also accidentally violated a restraining order, was used as evidence in court, accosted Spike Lee in a chicken suit, and was mistaken for Lady Gaga by a fan who might have had a copy of Catcher in the Rye. All and all, good times and a typical day in my life.

What advice would you give someone that just booked a TV appearance?

Two words: Have fun. You got this far, you earned it. Have a good time on set and bask in your success. However, don't rest on your laurels. Today's hard work and success might not carry over into tomorrow. So keep writing, keep getting onstage, and keep working hard. So celebrate like it's the best thing ever but continue to work as if it never happened because there is always more to learn.

Do you prefer forming jokes on paper or on stage?

Both. I am a writer first and foremost and have been writing since I could form words. My mother has all of my original stories, and I wish she would burn them for warmth in the cold PA winter. Just kidding. I write my jokes or ideas down on paper or even my iPhone so I don't lose them.

However, there are times I come up with some awesome bits either performing for friends or riffing onstage. It just comes out of my mouth as an afterthought and turns out it gets an applause break I never saw coming. That is when I write it down right away. Sometimes you find gold when you let go.

While one can find treasure while not looking, there is no substitute for a good, old fashioned notebook.

What do you like or dislike about comedy in New York?

My dislike is always the politics. It can harsh one's mellow, and also the grind associated with it. Additionally, there are so many comedians and so few spots and stage time is tough to get. But what I love is that the comedy scene is more like a community. Whenever you see another comic, even if you have only met once, they give you the big hello on the street. Also, as a newbie you get to appear on the same shows sometimes as people who are on national television on the regular which is not only cool to see, but an awesome way to network and get advice. And lest I forget people just love comedy.

There are times I have gone from spot to spot with a gaggle of friends and we spend the entire time dissecting joke after joke. Add in that I also get offstage with a new bit and there is someone waiting with a piece of paper and an alternate punch or tag, and sometimes it's what I have been missing all along. Not to mention once you find a good network they are amazing and are there for you to kvetch with, work on jokes, or whatever. Did I mention I get to do stand-up in the Greatest City in the World?

How does the reception of comedy abroad compare with what we have in the United States?

Different places have different expressions for things. Also, sometimes humor is just lost in translation from time to time. However, if you learn about your audience you will be very happy. So do your homework. And at the end of the day all anyone wants to do is laugh, and believe it or not any and all audiences are on your side. So if you are funny, they will give you what you want.

Who is the funniest person you know?

My family. My dad has the best one liners and my mom's rants are legendary. As for my sister, she is very honest and to the point which makes her funny, and my brother is a phenomenal storyteller. In my personal life that would be David Higgins. Enough said.

Why are jokes funny?

Because they are irony.

But also, they take the wind out of the sails of the things that are serious in life, the things that are taboo and lower our self-esteem. In comedy everyone is a target. Therefore, jokes are the great equalizer.

RICH CARUCCI

🐦 *@richcarucci*

The STEAMROLLER Of Comedy, Rich's quick wit and unique sense of humor make him a favorite in comedy clubs all over the tristate area.

Where did you grow up?

I grew up in Hackensack, NJ. I grew up in a nice area during a great time to be a kid. We had a lot of open undeveloped spaces where kids could go outside play, explore nature, climb, crawl and get dirty. We had drive-in movie theaters and Saturday matinees. It was a simpler, safer time.

What did your parents do for a living when you were a kid?

My parents both worked. Dad was a fireman who eventually became Chief; mom was a court reporter who owned her own court reporting school.

As a child, you appeared on several Chef Boyardee commericals, off-Broadway plays and the Ed Sullivan Show. What was that like? How did you get into acting?

As a child, we took regular visits to Palisades Amusement Park (closed Sept. 12, 1971). My two older sisters would enter the Little Miss America Contest there and won. The prize was to be in a real TV commercial. The day of the filming I went with my mom and sisters to watch. As I was sitting in the waiting room, a producer working on the commercial asked if I would like to also be in it. I figured why not, especially since it was a bunch of children singing Happy Birthday to a Gingerbread Man shaped pizza. I somehow got picked to do several more Chef Boyardee commercials.

I auditioned for several roles in stage, screen & TV over next few years. In 1971 I auditioned and got a part on The Ed Sullivan Easter Special "Clown Around" with Tiny Tim, Chuck McCann & Lucie Arnaz. My grandfather, Sebastian Carucci, was a vaudeville comedian, song & dance man and would come to Brooklyn everyday with me while filming. I continued to act in several plays and performed in various events for several years afterward but just went back to being a kid.

What was the first bit or joke you performed on stage as a comedian?

In the early '90s, my first marriage was failing and I wound up in Denver, Colorado. There, I decided to get back into performing; so I took some stand-up comedy classes. Stand-up had always been something I loved. My grandfather entertained us for years with his act. I seemed to excel at making people laugh since my days in catholic school to the displeasure of the nuns. I hung around Denver for a few years writing bits going to open mics and trying to deal with life's issues. I also had several articles I wrote and published. My marriage eventually crumbled and I moved back to New Jersey where I threw myself into finding a career outside of entertainment.

I met a beautiful young woman who inspired me to live my dreams. She thought I was wasting my talents and she was my biggest fan. She took me to several comedy clubs in NJ/NY Area and unbeknownst to me signed me up for a class at Stand Up NY. The class was slated to start a few months later but I wasted no time. I immediately started writing and going to mics, shows, watching, reading, eating and sleeping comedy. By the time the class started I had been back on stage dozens of times and had a lot of material in my arsenal. Mary Dimino (Award Winning

Actress, Comedian, Author) taught the class and became my mentor.

I started hanging at the clubs in NYC, daily, in early 2001 and got a job cleaning the NY Comedy Club every Thursday for one five-minute spot on a club show on a weeknight; usually around 11:30-ish for 4-to-5 drunk audience members who had not left yet. It didn't matter to me 'cause I was hooked. I scrubbed that club spotless: the toilets, the tables, chairs, the mirrors. I lined up the liquor bottles, took out the trash and put the food in the freezers. About this time a new form of comedian exploitation started called "barking," where a newer comedian is given flyers and set loose in Times Square and expected to stay out yelling and handing out flyers (mostly to tourists). Some clubs gave you a dollar per person you barked in, as well as one five-minute spot if you barked for at least an hour before the show.

Some clubs ran 6–7 shows every night, so I made it my mission to bark for every show I could, regardless. All the time holding down a full time job (911 Operator) sharing custody of two children and still cleaning the NY Comedy Club every Thursday. My first time on stage in NYC was the graduation show from The Stand Up NY class. It was a packed audience and all bringers and I went up in the middle. I actually did an Elvis bit and for 4 1/2 minutes I rocked the doors off that place. I was ready to quit my job and go to Hollywood. I got a tape of my performance and showed it to everyone.

Reality set in quick as every performance after that went bad.

If I had not had that tape of my first performance I most definitely would have crawled away for stand-up forever. I kept looking at it and thinking, 'What the heck?' I just kept working harder and harder and eventually started getting passed with bookers for paid road work. Gas was cheap and since I already had a good paying job outside of comedy, I was able to work all over the Tri-State area and not worry that I was making $50 and spending it all on traveling to and from the gigs. I did NYC Mon-

Thurs and every Sat & Sun I drove across countless miles to perform at private events.

Do you prefer forming jokes on paper or on stage?

I prefer to work out material in my head and on stage. I still go to open mics and I still do NYC on weeknights while doing paid work on weekends, but I'm starting to get more & more into writing everything down. I have a great writing partner (the beautiful woman who got me back into it), we are currently married & I still have the 911 job full-time. My daughter Amanda (20) graduated high school and moved to Boston while my son Rich (17) still lives with me.

How did you get the "Steamroller of Comedy" nickname?

I got the name Steamroller of Comedy from Tommy Hudson, a NYC based comedian who used to go by Tom Teska. I was performing at Gotham Comedy Club in 2002 when my material was bombing bad; the audience was yelling "You stink!" "Get off the stage" and "Kill yourself!" It was horrible. I was still new so I didn't yet realize how to perform different material for different audiences. I was panicking and the more they yelled, the dirtier my act got. I stayed up on stage and just keep rolling through it.

Somehow when I got off stage I had become a hero to the other comics because their butterflies had immediately disappeared; knowing no matter how bad it could possible go for them, no one was going to come close to bombing like I just had. Tommy Hudson said, "I can't believe you just kept going. It was like watching a Steamroller trying to roll over the audience."

Word spread of my disastrous bombing among the newer comics and of my ability to not let it affect me. They couldn't remember my name but they started referring to me as "The Steamroller."

What do you like or dislike about comedy in New York?

I love the comedy scene in NYC, but each club is different. In New York there are a lot of shows. They are everywhere any night of the week and some of the best ones are being produced in bars and restaurants that aren't regular comedy clubs. It's very hard to break into the regular clubs and an underground scene is running strong there. In NYC comedy is also turning into who's young and good looking, and who has TV or movie credits over who has talent. Comedians here are in constant danger of being exploited. Newer comics may not realize it; older comics have no other choice.

Who is the funniest person you know?

The funniest person I know was my grandfather. As for comedians, it was Otto Peterson of Otto & George fame. He was one of my best friends in the business and a true legend. I am a friend a fan of Rich Vos and also Nick Griffin. In my opinion, those are two of the best comics working today. The funniest un-comic person I know, I gotta say, is my wife Christine Borrelli Carucci.

STEPHEN SPINOLA

🐦 *@Mr_McStevie*

Born and raised in New York, Stephen is not James Franco despite the beliefs of many a crowd member. Stephen has had big dreams of being the most underrated Comedian of his generation since the age of six. He now lives those dreams while producing silly internet videos and performing live stand-up comedy all across North America, randomly wowing audiences overseas. Notable sites that have used Stephen's work include Playboy, Cheezburger, and The Huffington Post.

How does performing for theatre compare with performing on camera?

Performing in a theatre is way more difficult I find. There are no do-overs or takes. You feel like you have to get it right the first time. Not that you don't feel that way with film—you don't want to waste the time of the crew.

Bigger physical movements on a stage are more beneficial than on camera. It's tough to compare the results though. They are very different situations. Come see me perform live and compare that to one of my YouTube videos, it's just not the same.

Where did you grow up?

I grew up in the state of NY. I was born in Long Island but spent most of my childhood in Westchester.

What did your parents do for a living when you were a kid?

My dad was a lawyer and ended up becoming a Supreme Court Judge and the #1 Mediator in NY State. My step-dad traded stocks for a few different firms in NYC and Connecticut.

What was the first bit or joke you performed on stage?

The first bit that I performed on stage was about how my pee-pee is different from other people's pee-pees. The joke eventually evolved to become "I have a tattoo on my penis that says No Homo—that way when I have sex with guys it's not gay or anything."

How does the reception and/or practice of stand-up differ among cities around the U.S.? Where do you enjoy playing the most?

I think some cities have a more relaxed way of life and doing comedy, like Montreal, and some cities are more about the hustle and bustle and frustration, like NYC. I feel that I am generally well received in most cities, by audiences—not necessarily the comedians. I can think of some cities that just sucked and I didn't enjoy being in, but I can't think of any that had a truly poor reception to comedy.

Off nights and off crowds can happen in any city. I love performing in both Montreal and NYC but some other cities that I loved performing in were Eugene, OR—Seattle, WA—Vancouver, BC—Toronto, ON—Atlanta, GA—I also had the pleasure of performing in London, England a few times which was amazing.

You've appeared in Law & Order: SVU, Elementary & Slime Time Live. How do you prepare for a big audition?

Haha. There were no auditions for any of those roles. They were all extra roles that I put in my resumé as a joke. I think I had to go into an office to take 'headshots' for the first two, then somebody from that office called me a few days before the shoots

184

and was like, "Hey can you sit around for like 8 hours while we film stuff and then walk around in the background for 20 minutes?" And I was like, "Yeah." And the Slime Time Live experience was at Universal Studios in Orlando when I was really young. We signed up to be in the Live audience while walking around the theme park. My brother actually got pied in the face by Wee Man from Jackass during that show.

But to answer your question, the way I prepare for a big audition is I read the script and try to memorize some lines and then I smoke a whole bunch of weed about it. I spend more time preparing for the rejection after the audition.

Do you consider yourself a stoner comedian? If so, explain the plight of the stoner comedian. If not, my bad.

I don't really know. I am a stoner comedian because I am definitely a stoner and I definitely do a lot of stoner friendly material. I also do a lot of other material. I am also a white male comedian but I hope people don't think of it like that. I know they do, but I wish they didn't. I don't really consider myself anything but a comedian and an entertainer. Evan Jones and I do a weed themed show called the Cannaboiz so that doesn't help my position. As for the plight question—I think most people don't think white male stoners have any plight lol. Most comedians have their own individual plight regardless of their gender or skin color whether it be family issues or childhood experiences. There is no plight of a stoner comedian other than the plight of a comedian.

Comedy is an unfortunate situation, in general. I also don't think every comedian needs to have a plight. If you are a good writer and you make people laugh, you are doing your job as a comedian as far as I'm concerned. If you only want to be entertained by people with a plight, watch the Special Olympics— much greater chances you find what you are looking for.

Personally, my plight is having divorced parents, a crooked hand, and unrelenting anxiety. I am stoner because that is how I deal with my plight.

Do you prefer forming jokes on paper or on stage?

I usually don't form jokes on paper anymore. I used to write jokes with a setup and a punch but now I come up with a funny idea or a funny story and I just work it out on stage at open mics and come up with tags with my comedian friends. It's more organic and passionate. It's more "me."

How did you come up with the dick pics bit?

I was traveling the country in an RV when I came up with the idea. Dick pics were becoming very popular and I didn't really get the craze. I thought it would be funny if someone was sending out hand drawn sketches of their dick with beautiful scenery in the background. So I drew one for the scenery we'd seen that day. Then the next day I did another one. Then I got a shipment of 100 plastic cups in the mail that I didn't order. I ordered hair conditioner. But Amazon let me keep the cups.

So I made an online sweepstakes where if you sent me your name and address I would send you a hand-written letter with one of my newest jokes on it as well as a hand-drawn dick pic all inside of a plastic cup. So then people started sending me their addresses and I had to draw more dick pics to fulfill my promises. Some of them went to England and Canada. It cost about $140 to send them all out but I made a lot of people laugh and a lot of art in the process.

Who is the funniest person you know?

Justin Flanagan and Petey Deabreu. I don't know either of them very well but nobody makes me laugh the way they do.

Why are jokes funny?

Depends.

Words can have so many different meanings, it depends on how you interpret them. One joke can be funny to one person, and not funny to a whole different group of people. I think what makes a joke funny is that an idea diverges from your conventional way of thinking just enough that it doesn't make you upset.

DAVE ANTHONY

🐦 *@daveanthony*

Dave is an American stand-up comedian, writer, actor, and podcaster. He has lived and worked in San Francisco, New York City, and currently reside near Los Angeles. Dave has a podcast called The Dollop, which he co-hosts with comedian Gareth Reynolds. Dave is a regular actor and writer on Maron on IFC. He's also acted in many commercials and other television shows, including Arrested Development, The Office, and Men of a Certain Age. He has performed stand-up comedy on the Jimmy Kimmel Show, The Late Late Show, Comedy Central and a few other things that don't need to be mentioned because this is getting long.

How does comedy in New York compare with that in Los Angeles?

That's a hard one for me because I lived in New York so long ago. When I was there I think it was a lot worse. The audiences pushed people to be a bit dirty and they wanted ethnic jokes. It's changed a lot now—because there are more rooms besides comedy clubs to perform in. The clubs themselves are still not that good and I don't think they help you create a unique and smart act.

I think LA pushes you to be more of yourself, quicker. You get less stage time but I think that stage time is more worthwhile than in NY; when out in LA tend to do more story telling than bits. That's because the audience is allowing you to be more free.

Where did you grow up?

Marin County, California

What's interesting or uninteresting about Marin County?

It's super rich and I was poor. Big famous hippie area. Robin Williams was from there, so that was a big deal to me growing up.

What did your parents do for a living when you were a kid?

Dad a lawyer, mom a hair dresser.

When did you first want to start performing comedy? What was the first joke or bit you tried on stage?

1989. I cannot remember my first set. There was a joke about a going to the grocery store with a weird shopping list.

Do you prefer forming jokes on paper or on stage?

On stage.

When and where did you become a regular? What is the process of transitioning from open mics into paid sets?

I became a regular at a place called the Holy City Zoo in San Francisco. It was a pretty famous place where a lot of great comics got their start. It's a long and difficult process, or it was back then. First you had to slowly build up your set at the open mics, which were pretty much just at comedy clubs back then. You would slowly get better and better slots at the comedy club until you were considered one of the best open mic'ers.

At that point, you would start hanging out on non-open mic nights at the comedy club and asking for work. Eventually you'd get it and you had to make it work or you wouldn't get work again for a while.

What is the story behind The Dollop? What do you enjoy most about podcasting?

I was doing another podcast called Walking The Room. That was just me and another comic talking to each other about our lives. After a while, I stopped wanting to talk about myself so much and I wanted more privacy. I met Gareth on another podcast, called The Naughty Show. I thought he was really funny and wanted to have him on my old podcast as a guest. At the same time, I was planning on doing The Dollop.

My original plan was to have different comedians on every week and I would read them a story from history. I don't know where the idea came from, just thought it up one day. Gareth ended up coming on my old podcast as a guest host when the other host was out of town. And I liked him so much, I asked him to do the first episode of Dollop. After the first episode, I knew that was the show and I should only do it with him.

How did you and Marc Maron first link up?

I met Marc in SF in the early '90s when we were both living there doing stand-up. He lived there for a few years. We just kind of hit it off because we both were a bit angry and antagonistic. Marc and I have a very good understanding of who each other is and who we are. We don't tend to get offended by each other and there's no weird power struggle.

We both just want something to be funny and try to figure out the best way to get there. We are both used to talking stuff out as comedians, so that helps us to work together in the writing room.

The promo for your album, Shame Chamber, is very unique (and disturbing). How did you get the idea for it?

I was on Twitter and a comedian from Ireland named David O'Doherty posted a video of an Irish musician. In the video, he was in different locations out in nature, singing a song. I thought that would be an interesting idea to do for a stand up video.

Thought it might stand out, so I called a friend who knows his way around a camera and we shot it in a day.

What advice would you give a comic that's performing on TV?

Don't ever worry about it not being good. You've made it there for a reason. Just relax and be yourself. Try to let your personality shine through. You will not remember anything about the first TV set you perform. It just flies by and you can't remember anything. Try to have fun, though that is hard.

Who is the funniest person you know?

Gareth Reynolds.

Why are jokes funny?

Oof. There really isn't a specific reason.

There is just a combination of words that you can put together that causes people to have a physical reaction. To be honest, I don't want to know the answer to that question.

TED ALEXANDRO

🐦 *@tedalexandro*

Ted has performed on David Letterman, Conan O'Brien, Jimmy Kimmel, Craig Ferguson, The View and two half-hour specials on Comedy Central. Ted opened for Louis C.K. at Carnegie Hall and for Jim Gaffigan at Madison Square Garden. He has performed internationally in Jordan, Egypt, Kuwait, Hong Kong, South Korea, Singapore, Jakarta, England, Holland, Israel, South Africa and Qatar. He has starred on "Louie," "Inside Amy Schumer," "Oz" and "Dr. Katz". Ted also co-created the award-winning comedy web series "Teachers Lounge" with Hollis James. The series stars Ted and Hollis as a music teacher and janitor, respectively, in a NYC elementary school.

How will you react if the Mets win the World Series?

The last time they won was my senior year of high school. That was euphoric, especially the way that they came back on the Red Sox to win. It's hard to believe but it's almost thirty years later. So there's a certain amount of nostalgia and life inventory that accompanies a run like this.

That said, I'm enjoying the hell out of this and it makes me feel like a kid again. I'm sure I'll go nuts if they win.

Where did you grow up?

I grew up in Bellerose, NY which is in Queens.

What's interesting or uninteresting about Queens?

Queens is interesting because it's hailed as the most diverse county in the United States.

What did your parents do for a living when you were a kid?

My mom was a stay at home mother, raising five kids. She later taught high school religion, health and sex education. My dad taught in Bushwick for thirty years at an elementary school. He also caddied at a golf course during summers.

Why did you first want to start performing comedy? What was the first joke or bit you tried on stage?

I always loved stand-up comedy. My parents had a lot of classic albums; stuff by Bill Cosby, George Carlin, Flip Wilson, Steve Martin, Woody Allen. I absorbed a lot of great comedy throughout childhood and it stuck with me.

I did a lot of acting and sketch comedy throughout HS and college. I started going to open mics with my friend, Hollis James, after graduating Queens College. We performed as a duo for about a year. Then I started going out on my own. I wanted to try it as a solo act. One of my earliest jokes was, "I often think about my future wife, and how lax she's been about getting in touch with me."

Can you talk about the transition from doing open mics into becoming a paid regular?

It took me a couple of years to go from open mics to getting some paid work. I think change, by and large, is incremental. Sometimes you'll have leaps but mostly it's about working steadily, getting up every night, writing new stuff, taking risks, developing your style. Without realizing it, all of those muscles continue getting stronger.

If you're expecting life to change overnight, it doesn't really. Once you commit to a life in comedy, you take the ride and I recommend being patient and appreciating all of the steps and friendships along the way.

You've been a guest and performed on several late night talk shows. What advice would you give a comedian that is going to make his or her first appearance on TV?

First off, I'd say, "Congratulations." Getting a TV spot is exciting and the culmination of a lot of work. Before I got my first Letterman appearance I would study my favorites. I'd watch their sets on video or DVD (this was pre-YouTube). I would take notes, watching their body language, facial expressions, their vocal inflections. I'd even watch their performances with the volume muted, just to analyze the non-verbal communication.

I think with any artistic endeavor, preparation is important. Then over time you eventually get to a point where you integrate all that and have your own style.

What was the inspiration behind Teacher's Lounge? Why do you and Hollis work well together?

Hollis and I have basically been best friends since meeting at Queens College. We did sketch comedy there and starting writing and performing together. Once I graduated, I was an elementary school music teacher for five years and Hollis was a janitor for a summer job. We had the idea for Teachers Lounge, combining elements of our experiences on those jobs. So we set the show in a teachers' lounge and brought in other comics like Jim Gaffigan, Lewis Black, Janeane Garofalo and Dave Attell to play faculty members.

How does the reception of stand up differ abroad compared to within the United States?

There's a genuine excitement for stand-up internationally that feels different because the art form is new to many of these places. In the States, people have consumed a lot more stand-up comedy so people are both savvy and perhaps a bit jaded at times.

What do you like or dislike about comedy in New York?

I started here and I've loved it from the get go. I love that the best comics in the world work here regularly. This is where they come to work, not to get a paycheck. The emphasis is on the art in NY. I've been fortunate to come up watching and learning from the best, as well as the influx of young talent year by year. What I dislike is that there are so many comics here now, exponentially more than when I started in the 90s, so there are a lot of free shows that are unpaid. I understand the need for that, comics wanting stage time, but I also believe that artists should be paid. If you're working the top clubs, you should be paid well.

Who is the funniest person you know?

Dave Chappelle might be the funniest comedian I've seen. He's just preternaturally gifted as a performer and a hilarious comic. Artists make it seem effortless, and he does that. My friend Gil might be the funniest person I know.

Why are jokes funny?

I don't really know. I don't think it's one thing.

I guess a lot of times there's an element of surprise or a twist that people don't see coming. Ideally it's a combination of great writing and great performance. But it's a mysterious thing. It's not like music where you're dealing with notes and chords.

CHRIS MILLHOUSE

🐦 @ChrisMillhouse

Chris is a stand-up comedian and writer who is a regular at Broadway Comedy Club, New York Comedy Club, Hollywood Improv and various other clubs in New York and Los Angeles.

Why did you first want to start performing comedy? What was the first joke or bit you tried on stage?

I was always the kid joking around in class, trying hard to make people laugh. Right out of college I was working in radio, and when I got my first on air DJ gig I would try jokes on the air (late at night). When the phone lines would light up with people telling me whatever I said was hilarious I knew I had to try stand up (plus I always loved watching Comedy Central). My first jokes were horrendous, I started with all short jokes. First one I think was about how on St Patrick's Day all my friends paid me to run around yelling "you'll never get me lucky charms." So dumb.

Where did you grow up?

I'm from Trumbull, Connecticut.

What's interesting or uninteresting about Connecticut?

Nothing— Connecticut is boring as shit. Nice place to raise a family, but not much else. My town had a mall, lake and was home to the Little League World Series Champs in '89. Those three things are our claims to fame.

What did your parents do for a living when you were a kid?

My mom was a single mom, she worked a full time job as a receptionist/assistant and went to school at night.

Do you prefer forming jokes on paper or on stage?

Both, on stage is where you find the footing of a joke and work on the presentation.

When and where did you become a regular? What is the process of transitioning from open mics into paid sets like?

First place that passed me was my home club, The Comedy Store in La Jolla. I can't remember the first paid club gig I got, but I think it was at the Improv in Irvine. NYC & LA comedy scenes are completely different. In my personal opinion, its way harder to become a paid regular in NYC. NYC makes you earn it and grind it out hard to prove yourself, and in LA there's only a little of that 'cause most shows in LA don't pay. I think my first paid spots in NYC were at Broadway Comedy Club six or seven years ago, I'm still a paid regular there today.

What's the Hot Action Comedy origin story?

When I first moved to LA almost eight years ago, it was very hard to get stage time. I was good at getting people out to shows, and didn't want to do bringer shows.

So I reached out to the Improvs in Hollywood & Irvine and somehow convinced them to give me a chance. And back then the economy was in a recession, so the Improvs let me give away free tickets which was key to getting audiences in the room. Eight years later, the show is still featured monthly at the Hollywood Improv, even when I'm not there. I host it when I'm in town, and it's great to have that stage time still to this day.

I love being able to showcase big names on that show, as well as funny up-and-coming comics you might not have heard of.

How does comedy in New York compare with that in LA?

NYC really makes you earn paid spots & grind out the scene here. You can also perform multiple clubs, bars, and mics in one night because the city is so big and there's so many clubs and bars here. In LA, having four shows in a week is considered a good week…in NYC that's the average you do in a night if you grind it out.

NYC is the best stand-up comedy scene that's true to the art form. Audiences here are amazing, most of the clubs have small rooms with low ceilings that provide a more intimate experience. In LA, there are some very funny comedians, however there's also a lot of actors trying to be stand ups because their agents want them to do it.

There's also a lot of what I call "gimmicky comedy" meaning I there's a lot of comedians that use things on stage like beat boxing, singing, etc. and don't stay true to the actual stand up art form. I'm not saying that stuff isn't funny, it's just not true stand up. NYC has true stand up, and those other type of comedians don't really exist here.

How often do you think about Millhouse from The Simpsons?

I mean, I relate to him on so many levels obviously. Plus, every time I orgasm I scream "Everything's Coming Up Millhouse!"

Who is the funniest person you know?

I mean, I know so many comedians so that' s a long list. Favorite comic to watch is definitely Bill Burr, I don't know him that well but it doesn't get much better than him.

Why are jokes funny?

Jokes are funniest when they're relatable, in my opinion.

Or if they are well told, so you paint a great picture for the audience. There are some great story telling comics out there that are brilliant.

JONO ZALAY

@JonoZalay

Several years ago Jono moved from San Diego to Boston to pursue stand-up. He quickly became a staple in the New England comedy scene, while simultaneously earning his Doctorate in Neuroscience (he gave cocaine to rats). Since dropping his science hobby to pursue stand-up full time, Jono has been invited to perform in the Bridgetown, Limestone and New York Comedy Festivals. Jono now lives in New York City where he has been featured in Time Out New York and the Final Four of Caroline's March Comedy Madness. His background in science brings a unique perspective to his stand-up and provides the insight for his popular comedy-science podcast Universe City.

Is there anything from your training in science that you've brought into your career as a comedian?

Well there is an empirical nature to comedy: You try jokes you think are funny, but ultimately they need to be tested over and over before you can add them to your act. There is also a cognitive element to the logic in classic joke structure. That is grounded in science. Plus, I gave cocaine to rats. Comedy gold.

What's your name and where did you grow up?

Jono Zalay, San Diego CA. Formerly Jonathan Szalay [Jono is a nickname I got at age 11, and Zalay is the phonetic spelling (the "S" was too Hollywood for my gritty comedy brand)]

What's interesting or uninteresting about San Diego?

It's the nicest place probably in the world. Which is why comedy suffers so much there.

What did your parents do for a living when you were a kid?

They were both teachers.

Why did you first want to start performing comedy? What was the first joke or bit you tried on stage?

I felt compelled to find an outlet for the surplus of wacky ideas in my head. When I discovered there was a comedy open mic at the Comedy Store in San Diego, I signed up the next week. The first joke I can actually remember was around the holidays, I brought up two empty boxes in wrapping paper, and said "Hey check it out every body, I got Stage Presents. I was booed mercilessly and berated by the host. I found out years later a paid regular was cleaning up after the show, opened the boxes, found them to be empty, took it to be a metaphor for life, smashed the boxes with the mic stand, breaking it, was banned from the Comedy Store and quit comedy.

It seems like you've performed all across the United States. Can you talk about the transition from doing open mics to doing paid sets?

There is a delusion to most comics. You always think you are a little better than you actually are. That false confidence is sometimes necessary to pursue opportunities in the next level. When I moved to Boston from San Diego after a year and half of open mics, I thought I had 20 minutes of solid material. I probably had four.

But I kept hustling and showcasing for better and better gigs. By the time I actually got them I had become better. There is also an ever-escalating career ambition. My first goal in comedy was to get "passed" by a club. By the time I was, my goal was to get paid to MC, then feature, then headline, then TV and so forth. So while it keeps you motivated, it also makes you appreciate your current accomplishments less. Since you always want more.

How did Universe City podcast first start? How did you, Joe and Raj get together?

Joe Zimmerman and I had been friends following several comedy festivals when I was still living in Boston. He is very interested in science. Raj and I both have our doctorates (Raj has his in Microbiology). So when Raj and I moved to NYC around the same time, Joe approached us about a science-comedy podcast. Seemed like a natural fit considering our mutual friendship and interests.

Correct me if I'm wrong, but did you perform at The Naked Comedy Show at The Creek & The Cave in Long Island City? If so- what was that night like?

Sure did. I also used to perform naked regularly at the original Naked Comedy Show in Cambridge when I lived in Boston. It's some of my favorite stage time. The audience is totally disarmed so you can experiment with your material more than you could at a traditional standup show. It certainly keeps the audience engaged in the performance.

Why did you grow a double-mustache?

When you can grow facial hair like I can (my face is like a full canvas of beard hair within a month) it is natural to experiment with different configurations. So one day I shaved it into the legendary double mustache, where the hair went all the way around my mouth, and I thought it looked: 1) disgusting, and 2) hilarious. Jokes ensued.

What do you like or dislike about comedy in New York?

I like the amount of shows there are, and that the premium is on good joke writing. This scene has the best comics in the world, so you really have to raise your game, hustle, work hard and take some risks. It is as close to a meritocracy as you can find in comedy. It is also the broadest spectrum of quality in the world, so with the amazing clubs comes some of the worst shows that have ever cursed humanity. So you have to be unflappable. This scene has chewed up some promising comics. You can't feel too much, or it will really get you down.

Who is the funniest person you know?

Great question. Of the comics that I "know," probably Gary Gulman. He is the among the best pure joke writers in comedy. Of the ones whom I consider friends, I'd say Nick Vatterott and Dan Boulger. Nick has every tool a comic could want. Great joke writing, physicality, absurdism, likability. And Dan just speaks in material. He's forgotten more great lines and jokes than most will ever write.

Why are jokes funny?

Pure alchemy.

If you are referring to comedy theory, I think the most recent published literature on the subject is pretty close to true: The Hurley model of cognitive debugging and The Humor Code model of Benign Violation. Though both are repackaged versions of incongruity theory. Raj and I have our own model that it is a combination of entanglement and engagement:

ANDREW SCHULZ

🐦 *@andrewschulz*

Andrew is a comedian who can be seen on IFC's Benders, The Brilliant
Idiots Podcast, MTV and MTV2. He performs nightly in New York City
at The Comedy Cellar, Stand Up NY, The Comic Strip Live and Eastville
Comedy Club.

Any thoughts on the Knicks this season?

We're gonna get the 3-seed. I know that's completely
unreasonable. But fuck it. I'm a Knicks fan. I'm
unreasonable.

What's your name and where did you grow up?

Andrew Schulz. Grew up in Manhattan, NYC

What's interesting or uninteresting about Manhattan?

It's boring to me but apparently it's the most amazing city in
the world. I find nature and that stuff way more fascinating. I
guess what I find interesting is city folk are the least capable of
survival of any human being. Everything about my life is
convenient. I haven't cooked a meal in six years. Starting a fire is
just as far-fetched to me as space travel.

What did your parents do for a living when you were a kid?

My parents owned a ballroom dance studio.

Why did you first want to start performing comedy? What was the first joke or bit you tried in onstage?

I didn't want to perform comedy. I always loved humor. Loved making people laugh. I was a big stand-up fan, but it wasn't until I was managing a restaurant that had a comedy night and one of the producers asked me to go on stage that I wanted to do it. I can't remember my first joke. I think it was something about Magic Johnson playing with HIV and averaging 18 points a game. My take was: how is he not averaging 100? Who's playing tough D on him? A million comics probably thought of that joke. But hey, I was green.

Guy Code has really done a lot for dude humor for the past few years. What does MTV do well that other networks don't?

MTV rarely hires established talent. They groom nobodies that they believe in into somebodies. It's cheaper!!! They've got to be responsible for more future stars than any other network.

What is the origin story behind The Brilliant Idiots podcast?

Charlamagne and I would argue/discuss shit all the time. Random ideas. He got approached about doing a podcast and asked me to do it. We just funneled our arguments into a two-hour discussion and sprinkled-in some man-rape banter and boom: Brilliant Idiots.

Benders is the first show I've seen about an intramural men's hockey team. How did you land the role of Paul Rosenberg?

I lied and said I knew shit about hockey. I had done some stuff with Apostle in the past. They are great guys. They let me audition and thank god I got it.

What's the hardest part about touring on the road as a comedian?

Loneliness. You're Denzel Washington in the Book of Eli. You're in a foreign city with no car and no friends. It gets lonely. I try and experience the city as much as possible. I'll hang out with fans, random people that come to shows. Anyone.

What do you like or dislike about comedy in New York?

I like the amount of stage time. I like the competition. You're following the best so you have to be that good. Sink or swim. It gets you good fast. I'm also from NY so living here and doing stand-up isn't as inspiring.

What's the dumbest superhero name you can think of?

Superman. It's so un creative. Not to mention he's not even a man. He's and alien. Everything is wrong.

Why are jokes funny?

They aren't. Most jokes are horrible.

People are funny and when they tell jokes they're funny. Funny people are also funny when they don't tell jokes. A joke is just a paintbrush. It takes someone funny to paint something beautiful. I hated how artsy that sounded. Ugh.

JOEL KIM BOOSTER

@ihatejoelkim

Joel is a Chicago bred, Brooklyn based comedian and writer. He cares deeply about cats, appointment television, various feuds and more! He has been featured on Conan, Logo, Comedy Central and he desperately wants you to like him. Face drawn by Angelica Blevins.

What's the toughest part of getting a play from script to stage?

Collaborating is a real bitch, but was also probably the best thing to happen to that script. Over the span of one year I wrote 13 different drafts of that script, at one point starting completely over. Sarah made me kill a lot of darlings, which is tough. Lots of jokes and moments that I loved but she knew just didn't work.

You don't see it while you're writing, but you need that person outside of the script to be your eyes and argue with you about your words. It ultimately made for one of the best things I've ever written.

Where did you grow up?

I grew up in Plainfield, IL. A tiny Chicago suburb that is exactly what you imagine it to be.

What's interesting or uninteresting about Plainfield?

Plainfield is fairly undistinguishable from any other Southwest suburb of Chicago. Of course, there were always rumors that it was founded by the KKK, so I guess that's pretty interesting, depending on how you define that word.

What did your parents do for a living when you were a kid?

My dad was and still is an engineer for CASE IH, an agricultural equipment brand. He breaks new tractors for a living, which I swear is less exciting than it sounds.

My mom was a home health nurse, and she always brought home stray pets, so it was way more exciting than it sounds.

Why did you first want to start performing comedy? What was the first joke or bit you tried on stage?

I moved to Chicago, in part, to act; and I remember being very frustrated with the roles I was being offered both on camera and on stage. I was honestly just so fed up with getting called in to be IT guys or Chinese food delivery boys, and I remember I was working on a play for the New Colony at the time with Beth Stelling before she moved to LA, and half-heartedly brought up the idea of doing stand-up as a way to create material for myself. It terrified me, but she gave me some advice, and I eventually did it for the first time in front of a bunch of people at a variety show that the New Colony produced.

I'm not exactly sure what is technically the first joke I ever tried out, but I believe it was probably one where I compared being gay and Asian to fucking different kinds of dogs. It killed.

You're a playwright, as well as a comedian. How did you create Kate and Same Are Not Breaking Up?

I was working on pitching a few ideas to The New Colony with my friend and collaborator Sarah Gitenstein, and we had met a few times to discuss a bunch of ideas I had but none of them felt quite right. And then Amy Poehler and Will Arnett broke up and my Facebook feed exploded. People were freaking out and saying things like, "I don't even believe in love anymore." I've always found that kind of hyperbole sort of funny, and I remember texting Sarah: "A celebrity couple breaks up but gets kidnapped by a crazed fan and forced into couples therapy" and she said "yes" and that was pretty much it.

What is Live on Broadgay and why is it important?

Live in on Broadgay is a project created by two very smart and creative comedians Bowen Yang and Sam Taggart. They gathered some of New York's best gay comedians (and Jo Firestone) together and produced a fully staged adaptation of an episode of Sex and the City at an off-Broadway theater. It was one of the funniest things I've ever gotten to be a part of, will always remain as one of my fondest memories performing in New York and is in no way important.

How did Kam Kardashian originate?

Kam was the brainchild of (now) LA-based filmmakers Ryan Logan and Fawzia Mirza. They had both collaborated a ton, and wanted to do something more comedic. They brought me on in Season 2 to sort of expand the universe a little bit, and I got to play Kam's much put upon intern. I also wrote an episode and co-wrote a few more and had a blast.

What do you like or dislike about comedy in New York?

I love that the New York comedy scene is so big—there is an audience for really everything and everyone. There are so many people here doing some truly experimental, wild shit, that also happens to be super funny. It pushes you to do more, be funnier. Being around all that greatness can totally fuck with you too, though. Everyone is booking this or that, or getting a pilot greenlit.

If you focus on what you're not getting, it can lead to a lot of days spent in your bed in the throes of an existential crisis.

Why are jokes funny?

Good jokes, to me at least, give voice to those intangible thoughts and feelings that have been knocking around in your head.

Sometimes you laugh and don't know why, sure—but my favorite laughs have always been accompanied by a "holy shit—yes. Exactly! That. That is how I've always felt about hamburgers."

ADAM COZENS

Thought by some, but not all, members of his immediate family to be one of the best stand-up comedians working today, Seattle-native Adam Cozens is a thoughtful and engaging comedy talent who has been heralded by his peers as one of the best joke writers on the scene today.

What did your parents do for a living when you were a kid?

My mom was a secretary and personal assistant for a successful author and my dad worked a variety of jobs. He was a basketball player when I was a kid and was drafted into the NBA by the Portland Trailblazers. He later worked in grocery stores and in corporate for Eddie Bauer and Safeway.

He currently works at a really cool local mom and pop appliance store in their neighborhood. He can walk to work if he wants. Not a bad gig.

What's interesting or uninteresting about Seattle?

The actual neighborhood I grew up in is called West Seattle, which is in Seattle proper, but feels like a small town. Eddie Vedder from Pearl Jam lives in the area and drives his little red pick-up truck to the record shop. Most of the people I went to high school with still live in the area.

Which could be good or bad depending on your mindset. I love the community, but am also glad I got out. It can be very comfortable and hard to get out of the bubble.

Why did you first want to start performing comedy? What was the first joke or bit you tried on stage?

Well I originally wanted to just be a comedy writer and many of my favorite comedy writers got their start in stand up so I thought I should be like them and try stand up for a few weeks until the staff at 30 Rock snatched me up. Well, that didn't happen and in the process I discovered that I love performing comedy just as much as I liked writing it. I can't remember my first joke off the top of my head but I remember it was on Wednesday, March 31st, 2008 at the New York Comedy Club. I went to their open mic at 5pm and I paid the guy running the list $5 to get five minutes of stage time.

I was so scared to do it. It's the reason I left Seattle to move to New York City in the first place and despite that, I still sat in my new, much more expensive than I was used to apartment and had near panic attacks about going on stage. But that is what I moved for. So I went and I did it. I probably lied a bunch about things I hadn't done that I thought other people would find to be funny. And then stuff about my big head. I used to have a lot of jokes about my head. I still do.

How do you think your background in radio has influenced your career in comedy?

Working in college radio and trying (unsuccessfully) to make a career as a radio DJ taught me to not be scared by the reach of my voice. If I had really thought about how many people had the potential to hear my voice when I was talking on air, it would have crippled me. Likewise, when I'm performing my dumb jokes in front of a sold-out, Saturday night, $25-a-ticket-plus-a-two-drink-minimum crowd, if I took a second to think about how many ears my words were about to go into and how much influence my actions have over people's enjoyment for the evening, I wouldn't be able to do it. That would be too much pressure. But through those early years in radio, I guess I learned to shut that all out and just do my job.

Those Funny or Die News Flash sequences is really clever. How did you first join the team?

Thanks! I love News Flash. I joined the team fairly early on. An old acquaintance of mine who I did stand up with a few teams got hired to be the head-writer of this new topical Funny Or Die project called News Flash. I have always loved and felt like I was good at writing topical jokes so I contacting him and sent him some recent writing samples of mine and a few weeks later I was a full-fledged contributor. I probably write 50–80 jokes a day for the site and maybe one or two get used. It's a great exercise and has trained me to be less precious about my words and just get my thoughts out. You can always go back and fix them later but step one if getting them out and onto the page. Another thing I like about News Flash, and topical jokes in general, is how they are truly a slice of history. I have jokes in my stand-up act that I have been doing for close to 5 years.

You can't do a topical joke that long (trust me, I've tried). Topical, late-night monologue-esque jokes in my opinion are such a powerful tool to take a story that is dreary and sad and discouraging and poke fun at it; make light of stories that are otherwise just terrible and depressing. These kind of jokes have the power to help the world perhaps share a collective, cathartic breath. We are really saving the world. Oof, that got preachy and lame. Feel free to edit all of that out.

What advice would you give a comedian that is trying to get his or her jokes on TV?

Write every day. Even if you have nothing to write for. The very funny comedian Jon Fisch used to have a great podcast called "In The Tank" and he once interviewed a writer for The Late Show with David Letterman named Matt Goldich (now writing at

Seth Myers). In their talk Goldich said that he used to write topical monologue jokes in his room by himself every day.

He made it part of his routine and got good at it. He wasn't sending them anywhere; he was just writing them for practice sake. And it paid off. When he heard of a position at Letterman opening up, when all of the other comics were trying to teach themselves how to write monologue jokes or get their brains back in sync, he was primed and ready and he got the job. I loved that philosophy and started doing it myself. It has paid off for me on many occasions. I should contact Matt and say thanks.

Also, write what you think is funny, but be willing to compromise. Don't be so in love with yourself and your jokes that you can't take criticism. I used to get absolutely crippled by rejection or even notes. Once I got past that, things got better for me. Be true to yourself, but also realize that you are your own biggest fan as well as critic. Outside opinions can help a ton. Find like-minded writers or comics and get more comfortable running ideas by then. Then when it comes time to run ideas by big-wigs it won't be as foreign to you.

Can you talk about the transition from open mics to becoming a paid regular?

It just takes lots of time and hard work. I wasn't a natural stand-up. I was "funny" but being a good stand-up is very different. It takes years. Don't get discouraged. Or get discouraged, but use that discouragement to make you get better. I did open mics exclusively (I still do them for practice in addition to clubs and shows) for many years. Just learning how to be funny on stage. Learning how to sell jokes, how to hold the mic—all of that stuff. It really was some of my most enjoyable memories. Being a paid regular at clubs and getting to send in avails and getting spots and getting paid to tell jokes, it's fantastic. It really is. But it's nothing if you don't have the years of hard work to look back on allowing you to appreciate it. If you get (paid spots) in your first year or two, it won't mean anything to you.

Plus, at open mics, you can struggle and no one cares. It's almost encouraged to do bad because that means you are writing new stuff and working it out. As it should be. I can't stand it when people "kill" with their best stuff at open mics. I mean, do whatever you want—it's your time, but I guess it just bugs me. Use the time to develop new ideas. Even if they suck. Take a chance. Because in a few years, when people are paying and getting a baby-sitter and planning their night around seeing you perform, you need to be funny. It's not an option. We all have bad nights where you are off or things don't go right, but in general, you can't phone it in. You are a professional entertainer. And you have a job to do. And that is to make people laugh.

What do you like or dislike about the comedy scene in Los Angeles? How does it compare with that in New York?

I really like the L.A. comedy scene. When I first moved here I had heard all of the standard "L.A. sucks!" and "Everyone in L.A. just wants to be an actor!" "They aren't real comics! Just wannabes!" and I can't argue with that enough. Are their comics in L.A. who want to be actors? Heck yea there are. You know where else there are comics who want to be actors? In New York. And that's not a slam against New York. Comics are allowed to have other interests outside of purely doing stand-up.

I loved starting in NYC and putting in my first five years there and I love going back there, but that's just a dated slam against L.A. I have personally found the L.A. comedy community to be much more welcoming and supportive then New York ever was for me. I made great life-long friends in NYC, but as a whole, I feel more welcomed and comfortable in L.A. Much of that I'm sure comes from me being more comfortable with myself when I first came here too. Of course there are the cool kids and cliques and such in L.A. too, but in general, everyone for the most part seems to get along and wants each other to succeed. In New York it was much more cut-throat. In L.A. there seems to be a group-thought of "if one of us succeeds, we all succeed." I know that sounds lame, but it's true. I think the talent in L.A. right now is incredible and I'm happy to be a part of it.

Who is the funniest person you know?

In the world? Probably my old roommate Devin. He is a dentist in Everett, WA. We were buddies in high school and later lived together when I first moved to New York. He was a groomsman in my wedding. Another groomsman from my wedding was Joe Machi and he is easily one of the funniest stand-ups I've ever seen. I know I'm biased because he is one of my best friends, but the guy is truly amazing. Brian Regan is also pretty good, I guess.

Why are jokes funny?

In short, because ordinary daily conversation is awful.

Do we all have interesting conversations once in a while? Sure, on occasion. But those are usually few and far between. I used to believe that I would engage in one truly interesting, worthwhile conversation every day. But the older I get, the more I realize the true number is closer to once a week (it's highly possible the company I keep contributes to this lack of stimulation; but that is a conversation for another day).

The rest of the time we speak is a useful utility in order to get by; or filler. And there is nothing worse than filler. Idle chit chat about the weather and current events. Oh, kill me. And that's why I think jokes help elevate interaction. Throwing a well-placed joke into an otherwise drab conversation can lift everyone's moods. It can turn a sad, somber moment into something worth laughing or smiling about. A joke can lift a stuffy business meeting into a true, community-building experience. Jokes have much value in our modern culture. With that said, I would also argue that, inherently, jokes in-and-of themselves are not funny. The humor comes from the joke teller. Two comedians, or really people in any walk of life can tell the exact same joke with the same words and same timing and one will kill with it and the other will get silence. Because it is intended for one person's voice and not the others. We've all heard unfunny people try to be funny. It's painful.

Bless them for trying, but watching someone TRY to be funny is one of the least funny things in the world. You can teach writing, you can teach stage presence, but at the end of the day, you can't teach funny. It has to be in you. You can give someone all of the words and all of the pointers and the perfect, killer, A+++ joke and if they don't have it in them, it won't work. So in that respect, jokes aren't funny. People are funny. Jokes are just a serious of assembled letters.

SARAH TIANA

@sarahtiana

Regular on @Midnight on Comedy Central, regular on Chelsea Lately, regular/writer on The Josh Wolf Show on CMT, regular at "ignoring red flags." Writer for Jeff Ross and The Burn, Host of the Roast of Justin Bieber Red Carpet, Host of the CMA's Red Carpet. These are the things you know about Sarah Tiana. But what you don't know is that Sarah Tiana has been a "working" comedian/ex-waitress in Los Angeles since 2003.

What's your name and where did you grow up?

Sarah Tiana, Calhoun, GA

What's interesting or uninteresting about Calhoun?

Calhoun is a really small town where nothing ever happens. We didn't get a "sit down" restaurant until I was 18 (Cracker Barrel) and to this day the coolest thing that ever happened in our town was when Bo Jackson got snowed in on the freeway during the blizzard of '93 and had to stay at the Holiday Inn on our exit.

What did your parents do for a living when you were a kid?

My mom worked for Henkel as an office manager and my dad owned a Pepperidge Farm distributorship (basically he had a cookie truck).

Why did you first want to start performing comedy? What was the first joke or bit you tried on stage?

I never wanted to be a comedian. I started on a dare after I had written one joke about a news story I saw in LA. Here it is: A guy in LA shot himself in the head with a nail gun yesterday, the nail went into his eye socket, up into his brain and he didn't feel a thing. He worked the whole day! No one could believe he never noticed it! But I was like, man, I wouldn't be able to feel 3 1/2 inches if I got nailed, so what's the big deal?

How did you end up playing Carmen on Reno 911!? That character started out as a web series, right?

The character started in my sketch comedy company, The Straitjacket Society. I got the audition and they told me to come in as a character and decide if that that character called the cops or if the cops were called on them. Carmen obviously would call the cops because she has no friends and will do anything to make people come and hang out with her. Jail is the perfect opportunity for her to finally get a roommate.

I had no idea the part would end up being on four episodes. It only took an hour and a half to shoot the whole thing. Crazy!

What was the inspiration behind Straightjacket Society?

It was designed as an inexpensive way for actors in LA to write their own content and finally get on stage. Most major sketch companies are expensive and you only get one show. But that doesn't work in a town where as soon as you say you're an actor people say, "Where can I see you perform?" If you don't have an answer you look like an idiot. Straitjacket gave actors and writers and funny people a consistent answer to that question.

What do you like or dislike about comedy in Los Angeles?

I hate that it doesn't have the street cred of the New York scene, even though most comics that live in NY eventually have to move to LA. The Comedy Store is by far one of the coolest places in the world to perform. I love that it's exclusive (which is what most people hate about it). But it doesn't play favorites and you have to work your ass off to become a member.

When I started comics would tell me to NOT perform there, because it was a "boys club" and it wasn't worth the time it took to get in. But that just made me want it more. I worked my ass off for six-and-a-half years to get in and when they put my name up on the wall in 2010 it was one of the proudest moments of my life. Now the "boys club" is basically just a bunch of guys I call my brothers.

Can you talk about the transition from doing open mics into becoming a paid regular?

Well, that's a long transition. You go from open mics to "bringer" shows to running your own show and then, maybe, you're ready to start showcasing to be a paid regular. For me I ran my own shows at The Comedy Store so I always had an excuse to be there. Stage time is the ultimate key, until you've bombed (unintentionally) 100 times you're not even close to being funny.

I thought for years I was ready to become a paid regular, but once I got passed I realized how far I still had to go to becoming even a little bit worthy of that stage.

You've performed overseas in a bunch of countries, including: Germany, Singapore, Afghanistan and Guam (among others). How does the reception of comedy abroad differ from that in the U.S.?

The men and women of the military are always a little more attentive and excited to see your show, it's a nice break from the monotony of being overseas. The shows overseas are no different from my shows in CONUS but they are more important to me.

I put more pressure on myself over there. I can have a bad show in Houston because chances are I will perform in Houston again. I can't have a bad show at a FOB in Afghanistan. I only got one shot there.

You've also written for the ESPY's and NFL on FOX and I can tell you're a passionate sports fan. Which team do you care the most about and why?

The answer to that used to be the Atlanta Braves, but as I've gotten older and started playing fantasy football I've become a bigger NFL fan than MLB. I still go to Braves games by myself, but the Falcons are the team I think about on a daily basis.

Who is the funniest person you know?

Jayson Thibalt (onstage and off)

Why are jokes funny?

Is this question a joke? Because it's not funny.

JOSH SNEED

🐦 @joshsneed

In 2004, Josh performed at the prestigious "Just For Laughs" Comedy Festival in Montreal and made his television debut on Comedy Central's Premium Blend. In 2007, Josh was chosen by Comedy Central to perform in their inaugural South Beach Comedy Festival. Later that year, Josh filmed his 30-minute Comedy Central Presents special. In 2008, Josh finished 2nd out of 100 of Comedy Central's top comedians in the Annual Stand-up Showdown Competition, and released an album on Comedy Central Records called "Unacceptable", which iTunes selected as one of the Top 10 comedy albums released.

You've opened for Dave Chappelle, Dane Cook, Bill Burr, Louis C.K. and others. What have you picked up from some of those guys?

Well those are the greats you've cherry-picked from. They all bring different things to the table as far as things I could learn. Chappelle: the ability to take the most mundane topics and turn them into comedy gold. Burr: the art of being prolific and churning out new, solid material. Cook: the work ethic of treating the art like a business and building your brand. C.K.: take risks and work hard and when your time comes, you'll be so polished that you'll knock it out of the park.

What's interesting or uninteresting about your hometown?

I grew up in a very small suburb. Everyone knew everyone. Only had 73 in my graduating class.

What did your parents do for a living when you were a kid?

My father worked for Kenner Toys (read: awesome for a kid) as a model maker. My mother worked for Procter & Gamble.

Why did you first want to start performing comedy?

I wanted to be on Saturday Night Live, but wasn't sure where to start. I was in a weird spot career & college-wise and decided to try an open mic. Fell in love with it immediately.

First bit I did was talking about how crazy the flea market was. It's the only place where "you can pick up Jägermeister, fireworks, and a cold sore in a single transaction".

Can you walk me through the day you performed on Comedy Central Presents? What was that day like?

I submit for a special and was turned down, then a few months later I opened for Greg Giraldo at the South Beach Comedy Festival and Doug Herzog, the president of Comedy Central, was in the audience. I think him liking my set helped me get approved the next time I submitted. The day of the taping was pretty chill. Went over for a sound check and got to see my set for the first time. I got some direction on where I'd walk out and then I just hung out until I had to go back and record the show. It was surreal, easily one of the highlights of my career.

What's the comedy scene like in Cincinnati?

I love the scene here now. So proud of what it's become. There weren't a lot of people doing it full time when I was coming up. Geographically you couldn't pick a better place to be a road comic. Dayton, Columbus, Cleveland, Toledo, Detroit, Pittsburgh, Indianapolis, Lexington, Louisville, Nashville... all less than four hours away driving. Then Chicago, St. Louis, Atlanta, just beyond that.

What's the hardest part about performing on the road?

At this point it's being away from my family. Very hard to leave a wife and four-year-old for any amount of time.

What are some of thing things you talk about on your new comedy album, Unsung Hero?

My wife was in the audience when I recorded my first album, but we hadn't met yet. My life changed almost immediately just after that, so "Unsung Hero" is basically everything that has happened since the night I recorded "Unacceptable."

Do you prefer forming jokes on paper or on stage? Why?

I prefer to do it on stage. I think it's more natural and less scripted that way. It forces me to craft the bit in how I would normally talk rather than overthinking it. Once I get the joke out a few times, I can then work on selecting the timing and exact verbiage.

Who is the funniest person you know?

Comedian: Robert Hawkins
Civilian: Mike Zilliox

What makes a joke funny?

I won't say it if I don't think it's funny.

There was a time when a laugh was more important than me being able to sleep at night. Now, I really try to put my touch on jokes and make them relatable. My only hope is that the overwhelming majority of the people I'm talking to agree with me when I present it as being funny. Then I can keep paying the bills.

SAM MORRIL

@sammorril

Sam, one of the fastest-rising stand-up comics in New York City, is also one of the best joke writers in the scene today. How do you know that's true? Because he is writing this bio, and he wouldn't lie about that to get extra work. He has been seen on Comedy Central's Adam Devine's House Party, "Conan" on TBS twice, and is a regular on Fox News' "Red Eye." He's also been on Last Comic Standing, @midnight, and Inside Amy Schumer. He recorded his debut album on Comedy Central records, which went to #1 on iTunes and he also released his very own half-hour Comedy Central special. You can see Sam regularly at The Comedy Cellar in New York City.

What's your name and where did you grow up?

Sam Morril. NYC.

What's interesting or uninteresting about New York?

I have to explain New York to you?

Why did you first want to start performing comedy? What was the first joke or bit you tried on stage?

When I was three, I had a chunk about Cats on Broadway, which my mom enjoyed. My first stage bit? I have no idea. It was probably terrible.

What advice would you give a comedian that is about to make his or her first appearance on TV?

Drink a lot of gin. Like a ton. Until you can't walk. That's where the funny is hiding.

What kind of things do you talk about on your new album?

I talk mostly about how the Jews killed Christ, but it's very punchline heavy.

Do you prefer forming jokes on paper or on stage? Why?

Paper is the gym, stage is the game. Both are necessary. I'm miserable onstage if I don't have enough new (material). Much of my mood is based on how many ideas are put to paper and how well I executed them onstage.

I enjoy both when they're going well.

A lot of jokes are getting stolen and repurposed online now, which is terribly insincere. What are your thoughts?

It's pretty sad, but that's the world we live in. No one seems to value the origin of a joke. To me, creativity is important, but few on Instagram give a shit. They'll just steal a bit from a late night set and repost it without giving credit to the comic who created that joke and honed it in a club.

These internet joke thieves are not only creatively and morally bankrupt, but some have over six million followers. People don't care that they're supporting comedy criminals. I think the existences of these "internet personalities" are hollow and sad, passing off the thoughts and creations of others as their own.

What do you like or dislike about the comedy scene in New York?

Sometimes I get burnt out in how many sets I do. Bouncing around in a cold winter can take it out of you physically and emotionally. I care a lot about what I do and I'm frustrated when I don't see improvement. A lot of the sets I do now though tend to be for foreigners who don't understand subtlety or my sense of humor. The British tend to like a dark joke though. That being said, this is a great city to become a better comic.

Who is the funniest person you know?

Rasheed Wallace. Good friend of mine.

Why are jokes funny?

Freud said jokes are funny because of the release of tension.

Simon Critchley, a professor said, "Humor takes place in that gap between the human and the inhuman, between the mechanical and the organic, the living and the dead. It's a negotiation between those categories: something we do every day."

I think a joke is funny because humor is essential for human survival. The way Jewish settlers used to play songs and sing together to survive cold winters, we need jokes to get through mental hardships. Life is tough, and jokes simplify things. For me, at least, they release stress and help me to make sense of things. There's something special about a good joke. It makes you feel good. Then you can quote it to your friends, and make them feel good. What's better than that?

JEFF DYE

🐦 *@jeffdye*

Jeff stars in NBC's new eclectic comedy adventure series "Better Late Than Never." He is a nationally touring comedian, actor, host, prankster and Bigfoot enthusiast. Raised in Seattle, this class clown started doing comedy at Giggles Comedy Club right out of high school and was first nationally recognized on NBC's "Last Comic Standing" where he finished third. Since then he has had two of his own shows on MTV ("Money From Strangers," "Numbnuts"), his own "Comedy Central Presents" special and stared on numerous other TV projects, including "Girl Code" and "Extreme Makeover: Home Edition."

What was the first joke or bit you tried on stage?

I've always wanted to be a comedian and was always the class clown; so I've been practicing this job since first grade. My first bit was about white noise, and like the other bits I tried that night, it all bombed. Not a single laugh. Not one.

Where did you grow up?

Seattle, Wash., and the surrounding Seattle areas.

What's interesting or uninteresting about Seattle?

I guess it's a great place for artists to grow up and the culture is very encouraging to people who want careers that are considered unusual in other areas of the world.

What did your parents do for a living when you were a kid?

My mom worked in collections at a medical office and my father rented machinery to both construction companies and the city.

You seem to have a great relationship with NBC. Why do you think you and the network make a good fit?

I think NBC, unlike other networks I've worked for in the past, really gets me. They understand my "voice" and what is unique about me. I'm simple, smiley and lovable. They aren't trying to get me to be edgy or sexy or cool because what I am is goofy and silly and playful. So they let me be me.

What advice would you give someone getting ready for his or her first television appearance?

It's the easiest and most common advice ever but it is truth: JUST BE YOU. Stick to your thoughts your ideas and your voice and you can't go wrong.

What's the toughest part about touring on the road?

I guess the distance between you and your friends or family. I've missed a lot of fun things, events, weddings (etc.) because being a comedian means being on the road on weekends. I even lost the love of my life Kim because of touring, but it's all part of counting the cost of following your dreams.

Do you prefer forming jokes on paper or on stage? Why?

Both. They are both great ways and there's no reason to choose one. I love the writing part daily and I love the stage joke molding nightly.

**What do you like or dislike about the comedy scene in Los Angeles?
How does it compare with Seattle?**

They are both good. But in Seattle, at least when I was there (eight years ago), it was very clicky. There were circles that were very exclusive and if you weren't in them they treated you shitty. The LA scheme is bigger and a little more approachable.

Who is the funniest person you know?

The funniest people I know are all my friends. I love them. Not all of them are comedians but my core group of buddies are the funniest people I know and we keep each other laughing every day. Also, I'm friends with a TV host named Charissa Thompson and she is for sure one of most naturally funny people I know sober and drunk.

Why are jokes funny?

This is a strange question.

I don't know, why are boobs good?
Why does pizza taste so good? They just are.

YANNIS PAPPAS

🐦 *@yannispappas*

Yannis Pappas is a stand-up comedian and current host of AOL's Original Series, *2 Point Lead.* He was the Co-Anchor of Fusion Live, a live, primetime, one-hour news magazine program which focused on current events, pop culture and satire. Fusion TV network launched in September 2013 as a joint venture of ABC and Univision. Yannis' Half Hour Comedy Central Special aired in June of 2014 and is available on Amazon, iTunes, ComedyCentral.com and whenever Comedy Central re-runs it. Yannis has also been featured on AXS TV, truTV's How To Be a Grown Up, VH1's Best Week Ever, Fox Business and Good Morning America on ABC.

What's the dumbest superhero name you can think of?

Superman. It's a lazy, dumb superhero man. It's like Great Man! The Best Guy! Outstanding Man! if you really think about it, Super Man is the generic brand of superhero. Wonder Woman is stupid for the same reason. I also think it's wrong that she doesn't make as much money as Superman.

They both do the same job and one gets all the credit.

Where did you grow up?

I grew up in Brooklyn, NY.

What do you like about Brooklyn?

I grew up in Park Slope, Brooklyn. When I grew up it felt very far away from the city. Nobody wanted to come to Brooklyn. I always wanted to leave NYC, but then when I came back after college, I realized what everyone realized. It is the best place to be.

Everyone just keeps coming here. The rest of the country is suburbs and suburbs suck. Unless you are a car. They are great for cars.

What did your parents do for a living when you were a kid?

My parents were lawyers. They had their own practice and my mother also worked for the United Nations. I met them a few times. They were always working.

Why did you first want to start performing comedy? What was the first joke or bit you tried on stage?

Making people laugh was something I could always do. I was always the funny one. I wanted to do it after I graduated because I did not want to do anything else.

The first joke: "I just graduated from the American University, I majored in history and minored in Literature, I went on a few job interviews and realized the only thing I am qualified for is a high school diploma."

What kind of tricks have you picked up as an anchor?

Always smile and be performing even when you are not saying anything. The camera picks up everything. If you are sitting there and scratch your face it looks like you are high on crack. The camera magnifies and exaggerates everything. If you are sitting talking to someone in person and scratch yourself nobody notices, but if you do it on TV, you look nervous or on crack.

Can you walk me through the day you filmed your Comedy Central special? What kind of things were on your mind?

Mostly I was thinking about how it was hard to find something good to eat in Boston. I spent the rest of the time trying to stay calm and keep negative thoughts out. Just like most days. Comics usually hate ourselves a bit because we have the decency to see ourselves for what we really are.

What effect did Donnell Rawlings have on your career when you were a younger comic?

Donnell was the first professional comic who was really funny to tell me I was funny. He gave me opportunities and took me on the road when I didn't really understand what that was and wasn't really sure that you could make money doing stand-up comedy. We both are kind of do-it-yourself guys, so it was nice to see someone who was so proactive. He really gave me my start in 2006. That is when I really started doing comedy full time.

Do you prefer forming jokes on paper or on stage? Why?

I never write on the paper. I just babble and hope there are some laughs somewhere.

What do you like or dislike about comedy in New York?

I like that the funniest comedians in the world are here are came up here. Dislike: Too many straight, white, male comics. As one, I apologize for this.

Who is the funniest person you know?

It could be any of my friends on any given night. I am friends with the funniest people in the world. It's one of the perks of doing this for a living.

Why are jokes funny?

They aren't. It's not nice to tell jokes, they hurt people's feelings.

MYQ KAPLAN

🐦 *@myqkaplan*

Myq is a comedian named Mike Kaplan (pronounced "Mike"). He is a 2010 Last Comic Standing Finalist and has appeared on the Tonight Show with Conan O'Brien, the Late Show with David Letterman, Comedy Central Presents, and all the other places he's been. You can listen to Myq's podcast, Hang Out With Me, on the Keith and The Girl network. His debut CD, Vegan Mind Meld, was one of iTunes' top ten best-selling comedy albums in 2010, followed by Meat Robot in 2013 and his one-hour Netflix special Small Dork and Handsome in 2014.

What kind of decisions go into putting together a special? What did you enjoy about the process of creating Small, Dork & Handsome?

The thing I love most about comedy is writing and performing and honing and aiming to perfect new funny ideas; new jokes. Putting together a special is also fun, but it's on the other end of the spectrum. Taking jokes that have gone through that process and constructing/presenting them as a final product, a show. I like it all. I like the snowflake and the ice sculpture, or the avalanche. Of ice sculptures.

If you mean things like, how did I decide what the backdrop should be, or the lighting, mostly other people offered me options and I said "this one seems good." I care mostly about the comedy.

So, I decided to write jokes years ago, and then years later, a special happened.

What's your name and where did you grow up?

Legally Michael Kaplan. Illegally Myq Kaplan. I grew up in Livingston, NJ, then Upper Saddle River, NJ; then Allendale, NJ, then college in Waltham, MA; then Boston, MA, now Brooklyn, NY (I'm still growing!).

What's interesting or uninteresting about your hometown?

I grew up in the suburbs of New Jersey! New Jersey is right near New York City! That's interesting by proxy! Or uninteresting on its face.

What did you parents do for a living when you were a kid?

My parents were both music teachers.

When did you realize you could be a comedian? What was the first joke or bit you tried on stage?

I realize it every day. But also... I realized I could be a comedian after I'd been doing comedy for some time. (I was initially striving to be a singer-songwriter, and I played some funny songs at a comedy club occasionally. In between the songs I would talk, and realized it was fun to make people laugh with words and not music, in addition to words and music. So, I was doing comedy before I realized I could do it.) And I realize it every day. One of my first jokes was something like this: "Did you know that Philadelphia used to be called Liberty Bell Town, but that didn't have quite the right ring to it?"

Last Comic Standing seems like a real launching pad for comics. How has the show impacted your career?

Most career advancement in comedy is gradual these days for most people. Last Comic Standing was the biggest non-gradual leap forward in people seeing my comedy and knowing who I am. Millions of people watched every week, and after the season ended, I was able to perform at a higher quantity and quality of comedy venue because I had become more of a draw than I was before. (Before, I was basically not a draw, and after, I was MORE than not.) To this day, there are almost always people at my shows who are there because they first saw me on Last Comic Standing, for sure.

You're also a veteran of late night performances. What advice would you give a comedian that's going to make his or her first appearance on TV?

Have a good time! Don't worry about this, or anything, because eventually we are all ash and dust.

(That's perfect) What's the origin story behind the Hang Out with Me podcast?

A guy emailed me and said "want to be a part of a new podcast network I'm starting?" and I didn't know who he was, so I said thanks but no thanks. So I thought about starting a podcast and seeing if I could get it produced by a network I'd heard of, like Nerdist or Earwolf. I looked into it and ultimately determined that to start out, I'd have to do it on my own. Or... with the guy I'd never heard of. So I went back to him and said "sure!" and started making podcasts. Then eventually that guy decided to get out of the podcast producing game, and I reached out to my friends Keith and The Girl, who were expanding their podcast empire into a larger network, and now it's there.

That's the logistical origin story. The emotional one is this: I'd been a guest on a lot of people's podcasts, and it was always a blast, just hanging out with friends, talking. I remember a specific day where I had been in a less than great mood pre-podcast, and then after I felt so good, that I was like "I should do this more often! Not just when people invite me to do THEIR podcasts... I could have my own!"

And that's how Hang Out With Me was born.

Do you prefer forming jokes on paper or on stage? Why?

I like forming jokes in any way they form. My process usually begins with an idea that I speak into a digital recorder. After that, I write it down into a notebook, and after that I type it into a computer. All the while, I'm also saying it on stage, adding to it, editing it, tagging it, riffing other ideas, and those ideas go through the same recorder-notebook-computer process. So, if I had to choose JUST writing on stage or writing on paper, I would choose the stage, because that is where standup comedy happens. But I don't have to choose. I can do everything. (Also sometimes, jokes can arise from writing alone, like if I'm writing an email to a friend and something funny comes out. I'm open to that as well, but the process for me usually begins with speaking out loud.)

What do you like or dislike about comedy in New York?

I love how big and diverse and multi-faceted it is. Any given night, there are so many fun shows going on, so many comedians, so many friends and potential friends, so many audiences… New York has such a large quantity of everything, that it statistically makes sense that it has so much in the way of quality as well. (Of course, a pessimist might say that with so much of everything, there's also so much more negative as well as positive, and that's true, but I prefer to focus on the positive. You can't experience everything all the time, so why not pick and choose what makes you feel better, when possible.)

Who is the funniest person you know?

I can't name just one funniest person. I know so many wonderfully hilarious comedians and humans and human comedians (and maybe others), that if I were to start naming them, I'd leave some out for sure… so I'll just say my girlfriend Kasey for now, because she's here.

Okay, you forced my hand… here are SOME candidates for some of the funniest people I know: Henry Phillips, Zach Sherwin, Gaby Dunn, Micah Sherman, Rebecca Drysdale, Aparna Nancherla, Baron Vaughn, Nick Vatterott, Reggie Watts, Gary Gulman, Kate Berlant, Rory Scovel, Ramin Nazer, Ben Seidman, Paul F. Tompkins, Doug Stanhope, Maria Bamford, Jackie Kashian, Renata Tutko, Shane Mauss, Josh Gondelman, Ken Reid, Baratunde Thurston, Erin Judge, Ryan Singer, Matt Knudsen, Brent Weinbach, Brandon Scott Wolf, Paul Barman, Louis CK, Myka Fox, Wayne Federman, Mehran Khagani, Chris Gethard, Nikki Glaser, Pete Holmes, Kumail Nanjiani, David Huntsberger, Sabrina Jalees, Joe Karg, Joe List, Robert Mac, Amber Nelson, Adam Wade, Emo Philips, Julian McCullough, Colin Quinn, Giulia Rozzi, Abe Smith, Auggie Smith, Victor Varnado, The Walsh Brothers, and ALL OF MY FUNNY FRIENDS WHO I DIDN'T THINK OF IMMEDIATELY HERE SORRY FRIENDS YOU ARE ALSO THE FUNNIEST!

Why are jokes funny?

1) Because!
2) Why AREN'T jokes funny?
3) They're not. (Just kidding. They are.)
4) Because the people telling them are funny.
5) Science.
6) Religion?
7) Soup.
8) I'm hungry.
9) It's lunchtime.
10) List over.

DANI FERNANDEZ

🐦 *@danifernandez*

Dani is a stand-up comedian, writer, and host at Geek & Sundry. She began doing stand-up at open mics around Los Angeles near the end of 2013 and her first show was at The Comedy Store in 2014. She hosted at Comic Con in 2014 and 2015 and was a panelist at Comikaze in 2015. She has appeared in the Tournament of Nerds! show at the Upright Citizen's Brigade Theater in Los Angeles, California, alongside Dolph Ziggler.

When I Googled your name, a 23-year-old boyband singer from Spain showed up. How often do you think about that dude?

Occasionally. I am also, apparently, a talented magician. The boyband member blocked me on Twitter after I tweeted at him asking if I could buy his handle. I then, asked my followers to tweet at him and ask if I could buy his handle. In hindsight, probably not my best move.

I've been blocked by many Dani Fernandezes (Fernandezi?) on Facebook for repeatedly tagging them in my photos. It was an accident.

Where did you grow up?

I'm not sure where I grew up. I spent half my life in Southern California and the other in Texas. Most times people introduce me as being from San Diego because my whole family grew up there—but who knows!

What's interesting or uninteresting about those places?

San Diego and Texas are oddly similar. A lot of rich people living in the suburbs. Very conservative in parts yet it has its wild side. I went to school at UT in Austin—that's about as crazy and liberal as you can get in the south, and I loved it. They have a motto "Keep Austin Weird" and they really did.

We had a famous homeless man as the town mascot, my roommate used to drunkenly throw vodka bottles off our balcony onto party goers below and there's a brownie delivery service that will bring milk and cookies to you in the library while you study. I mean, the place was exciting (not the vodka bottle throwing part though).

What did your parents do for a living when you were a kid?

My father worked in advertising and my mother worked for KinderCare (a popular daycare). My father's business was very Mad Men-esque. Lots of women, hard liquor, cigars—I grew up around that. We moved around a lot, Kansas City, Orange County, San Diego, Dallas, Manhattan. He worked for Philip Morris (who owns Marlboro) in Manhattan and I remember being confused as to why daddy sold cigarettes when I learned in school that only bad people used cigarettes.

He would take us to their headquarters and let us pick out all the Lunchables we wanted (they owned Kraft), and I was sold.

Can you talk about the panel you were on at COMIC CON?

Although I had worked the floor and performed at many cons (yes I'm bragging) this was my FIRST EVER panel. I was so excited that people actually gave a shit about my opinion. We talked about possible Star Wars spoilers, my obsession with Dragon Ball Z, and women in comics. I remember arguing with my fellow panelist Clayton Thomas about when it's appropriate to interrupt a woman's day to hit on her (which is not at the gym when her ass is sweaty and she has wiped off all her makeup and she doesn't need your troll face trying to talk to her troll face while she does wind sprints on the treadmill) and about how he thought women shouldn't be too skinny. Some women are naturally skinny. I would love to be thinner, but I don't think that's a reason to shit on thinner women (unless it's some kind of weird website where they are being paid for it).

Which storyline are you most looking forward to in The Force Awakens?

Kylo Ren being Han and Leia's kid. I'm looking forward to the story of Han and Leia. They have chemistry, all these years later. It gives us all hope—some might say... A New Hope.

Do you prefer forming jokes on paper or on stage? Why?

Paper. I'm a writer first, comic second. I grew up writing, I was in the journalism program before switching majors at UT. I moved to LA to write. I then got a job at The Ice House Comedy Club so I could be around people I could sell my sketches to. And that's when I met comics who encouraged me to get on stage. I blame them for all of this.

makes sweeping motion to dirty apartment and low bank account balance

You've been open about living with an autoimmune disorder. How do you think it has had an effect on your comedy?

Immensely. I stopped performing every night. I'm also only two years in. When I started doing stand-up, everything took off. I was getting on shows, recording sketches for different comedy sites. I was doing roast battles, and making friends fast. I couldn't believe this was my new life. But then I got really sick.

My thyroid was the size of a tennis ball and all my hair started falling out. I remember leaving the hospital and getting a flat tire right before a show I had at Malo and I cried my eyes out on the phone with my mom in the car. She told me to go home and some of my friends did too. I remember thinking "what would a real comic do?" They wouldn't go home, they'd go in there and use this. I did the show and talked about how someone had a voodoo doll of me and was ruining my life.

It was great and extremely therapeutic. I figured all my sets would be like that. God I was naive as hell.

What was the inspiration behind Einsteinfeld?

The Historical Roasts, and roasts in general, are where you can push the envelope and be offensive, as long as it's creative. I was roasting Albert Einstein (Matthew Broussard) and knew they'd hit me with Mexican or Catholic jokes, so I wanted to get in some Jewish jokes without going the easy/stereotypical route. I said, "You're so Jewish, your best friend is George Costanza. If you were any more Jewish, you'd be Einsteinfeld."

We're in an era where it's the easiest it's ever been to steal someone else's jokes. Has it changed the way you present your humor?

Absolutely. If I think something is clever that I want to use on stage, there is no way in Hell I'm putting that on Twitter. The best way to claim a joke is to do it as much as possible on stage so that you are known for that joke. Sometimes I see things I have written (or others) where someone changes one or two words and claims it as their own. It's disappointing. It may seem stupid to get upset over posts and tweets but many of us make a living off our writing. I've gotten paid to tweet or sell jokes on many occasions. In this business, you kind of take what you can get. Most of us are poor broke comics and writers. If there's one misconception I'd like to set straight, it's that this life is glamourous. It's not.

What do you like or dislike about the comedy scene in LA?

I love that there are so many people and I hate that there are so many people. It's like—how are we all going to make it? Oh that's right—some of us won't. Just when you think you and your friends are doing well, there's a whole crop of people on the other side of town who are doing even better. There are a multitude of mics and shows every single night of the week. That's insane. A lot of places don't have that. I love that you can be on the same show as Andy Kindler, Chappelle, or Joe Rogan (or whoever your idols are). I love that despite there being so many terrible people here, you can actually find a family in comedy.

Who is the funniest person you know?

No one makes me giggle like my mother. She's an innocent, real life Debbie Downer. I remember the one episode of Oprah, years ago, when she gave everyone in her audience a car. I was in shock and somewhat jealous.

My mom stared blankly at the TV and said very matter-of-fact, "Odds are, someone will die in one of those."

Why are jokes funny?

They help us make light of the darkest moments in our lives.

NEEL NANDA

@NeelNanda

Starting comedy in Atlanta, GA and now based in Los Angeles, Neel Nanda has performed all over the country with some of comedies' biggest acts. Neel has acted and performed stand-up on Comedy Central's Adam Devine's House Party and VICELAND's Flophouse. He has appeared on IFC's Garfunkel and Oates and performed stand-up comedy on Oxygen's Funny Girls. You can catch Neel every week at his show on the Westside where he has shared the stage with comedians like Hannibal Buress, Demetri Martin, Laura Kightlinger, and even Yakov Smirnoff.

When did you realize you were funny?

When I was in middle school I was glued to Comedy Central. I would go home every day and watch hours of Premium Blend, Comic Remix and Comedy Central Presents. I used to sit down on the floor in front of my TV and write down every joke that I liked word for word so I could tell it to my friends at lunch at school the next day. I was 13, so I didn't realize that I was just stealing jokes for years.

When I got to high school I realized I needed to write my own jokes and I used the same notebook to start writing my own jokes based on the joke writing structure that I mimicked from all of my favorite joke writers. I started testing these jokes on friends and girlfriends who quickly became ex-girlfriends and eventually I decided I was funny enough to try it on stage in front of people. I performed my first open mic set when I was 19 and the set consisted of one-liner jokes I wrote in high school.

What did your parents do for a living when you were a kid?

My dad was a computer scientist until I was in middle school. We had just moved into a nice neighborhood, and less than three years later my dad was laid off. So I quickly became the poor kid in the dope neighborhood. My dad then opened a liquor store and we were broke for a long time, but at least I got free Red Bulls in high school.

My mom worked in a grocery store pharmacy where she got me my first job as a pharmacy technician when I was 15.

How does the comedy scene in Atlanta compare with that in LA?

The Atlanta comedy scene is incredible and continues to become more incredible every time I visit. Some of the strongest emerging comics in the country were once based out of Atlanta: Clayton English, Matt Broussard, Mia Jackson, Noah Gardenswartz, Rob Haze, Caleb Synan just to name a few. The thing I loved about doing comedy in Atlanta was that the open mics were generally packed with audience members who wanted to laugh; and, even if they weren't, the comedians were supportive and would listen and laugh if your joke was funny.

For this reason alone, Atlanta is an incredible place to write and develop material. Los Angeles also has an incredible group of comics that push you to be great. I've had countless sets in L.A. where I've had to follow a comic who I used to watch on television before I moved to L.A. At first it was intimidating, but after a while I started enjoying the challenge.

Stage time is tougher to get in LA so this city has forced me to start writing, acting, producing and directing. Even if I direct and produce something I'm not proud of I'm always happy that I at least gained some experience doing something comedy related that I enjoy.

Season 1 of Flophouse on VICELAND was one of my favorite things to watch. How did you get involved with the show?

It's actually a pretty uncommon story that a lot of people think is a common story. I was in San Francisco doing a set at Lost Weekend Video (one of my favorite spots that unfortunately no longer exists) and Lance Bangs (the director of Flophouse) was watching the show. Lance was in-town to tape the San Francisco episodes and I happened to be in-town at the same time.

He saw me perform that night and asked if I could be on the show the next day. I couldn't believe it. I had been a fan of Lance's work (mostly Jackass) and I even said, "Can you really do that?" and he replied, "Of course I can, I'm the director." and sure enough I did the episode the next day. I reconnected with Lance in L.A. about a month later and we talked briefly about doing an episode in Atlanta. Lance was definitely on the fence about Atlanta because he had other cities in mind, but I convinced him that Atlanta has one of the greatest comedy scenes in the country and he started planning an episode at The Hangar.

Can you walk me through your general joke-forming process? How do you form premises, build punchlines, etc.?

I walk around with a notebook and have a notebook next to my bed in case I think of a premise to jot down. Then I sit down and look at that material the next day and try to figure out how to tell it on stage. I don't always have stuff to jot down and I try to spend every day writing material so some days I just tag old material. I'll look back at my old material and reflect on what works and what doesn't work in the bit and try to punch it up accordingly.

I like to take a lot of time with my material. Some comics frown upon doing a lot of old material, but honestly I feel like some of my old material is never done because it evolves and becomes tighter every day. I generally keep my sets around 70-percent old and 30-percent new because I want to throw a sprinkle of my new material in to see if it'll be seamlessly strong in comparison to my old material. I'll also sometimes write on stage. Generally, if a new joke isn't working I will try to save it by riffing. Last week I was on stage doing a new bit and I was doing a joke that involved numbers and I found a funny mathematical comparison while I was on stage and so I just said it and it landed (which is one of the most incredible feelings) so now its permanently part of the joke.

How did Unnecessary Evil show at Westside Comedy Theater start?

My buddy/co-producer Tushar Singh was moving to Los Angeles and we had talked about starting a show together so I was looking around the city for venues. I had performed at the open mic at the Westside Comedy Theater a few times and had seen a few shows. I quickly fell in love with the venue. The stage, the seating, the bar and the location is perfect for a dope comedy show. I was hanging out at the theater one night before an open mic in order to inquire about booking a show at the venue. I was standing outside when a dude with a giant smile and a bigger mustache was hanging out right outside the door smoking a cigarette. I asked if he worked at the theater and he said yes and then we had a brief conversation about what I wanted to do at the theater and he after he finished his cigarette he told me he was one of the owners of the theater (Sean Casey). At the time the theater didn't produce many stand up shows and he was excited to bring more stand up to the theater.

We exchanged emails and when Tushar moved to LA we had a meeting in Sean's office and we picked some dates. We had no idea what we were doing but we somehow packed out each show and we starting booking more dates from there.

Why do you think comedians become comedians?

I think the traditional answer is narcissism or depression, but I'd like to think that comedians become comedians because they're fans of comedy. Like I mentioned before, I used to be glued to Comedy Central and when I first started writing jokes and I would watch a copious amount of stand-up on Comedy Central and whatever I could get my hands on online. I fell in love with Carlin at around 16 or 17 and I watched every one of his specials.

I still love Carlin because if you watch his specials chronologically you can see him grow as an artist and as a human being. His early specials are nothing like his later work and I've always appreciated how much he grew and adapted to each decade he was doing comedy in. I became a comedian because I loved the craft. I loved writing jokes and as soon as I started telling them I fell in love with that too. I feel like the comedy came before the narcissism and depression for me.

What advice would you give a comic that is trying to advance his or her career?

Keep your head down and focus on your jokes. Write every day and try to perform every night. Treat comedy like a job and it'll become a job.

What are you working on now?

I'm working on a lot of stuff that I'm keeping on the down low for now, but I'm also constantly working on my material.

What makes a joke funny?

Intent.

If your intent is to make a joke funny and you believe it's funny and you do everything to execute what you find funny about it then I think any subject matter can be funny. There has been a lot of "don't joke about this" or "don't joke about that" lately and I think if your true intent is to be funny you can make a joke about anything funny.

ADAM NEWMAN

🐦 @Adam_Newman

Adam Newman is a New Hampshire-born, Georgia-schooled, ex-Brooklyn-based, now LA-based comedian who has performed stand-up on the Late Show with David Letterman, John Oliver's New York Stand-Up Show, Gotham Comedy Live, and his own episode of Comedy Central's The Half Hour. He has also appeared on MTV's The CollegeHumor Show, HBO's Last Week Tonight and Silicon Valley, the Tyra Banks Show (weird!), Comics Unleashed, and is a regular contestant on Comedy Central's @midnight. Adam has released two critically acclaimed stand-up albums, Not for Horses (2011) and Killed (2015) through Rooftop Comedy Productions.

Where did you grow up?

I grew up in Bow, New Hampshire, but in the middle of high school my family moved to Marietta, Georgia. True story: My first day at my new high school, I had to stand up and introduce myself. I said, "Hi, my name is Adam, I just moved here from New England," and a girl raised her hand and said, "Then why don't you have a British accent?"

When did you realize you had to be a comedian?

I wanted to be a comedian for as long as I can remember, but after about a year of having a boring office job fresh out of college is when I decided I was actually going to go for it.

Can you walk me through your joke-writing process? (finding premises, forming punchlines, etc.)

I don't really have any consistent process for either of those two things. If something strikes me as funny, I write it down and try to talk it out it as soon as I can get on stage.

How has that process evolved over time?

I definitely used to write things out a lot more before trying them on stage when I first started. Over time, I've gotten more comfortable figuring it out in front of an audience.

How much material had you accumulated by the time you booked your TV-debut on Letterman?

Letterman actually wasn't my TV debut! I did John Oliver's NY Stand-Up Show on Comedy Central about a year earlier. IRREGARDLESSLY, I had already done an album and was headlining occasionally by the time I got Letterman, so I was pretty comfortable doing an hour at that point.

Is there anything that's especially difficult about putting together a special that people might not realize?

Nope. Easy as shit.

How does the comedy scene in New York compare with that in Los Angeles?

I've found both scenes to be great! There's no competing with the quantity of stage time available in New York, but in LA you might just find yourself performing for 300 people in someone's backyard with kiddie pools full of beer and a taco truck in the front yard.

How do you think a comic should find his or her particular style?

I think any comedian's best bet is to write and perform what makes them laugh the most, and figure out what of that they can make relatable to their audience.

Why doesn't Claire's do genital piercings?

My guess is either because they do their piercings in the window where the whole mall can see or the gun just can't handle it.

Any thoughts on LeBron winning the title last week?

If my Boston Celtics aren't going to win it, I root for my favorite players and/or stories. I like the LeBron story. I like that he came back and won one for Cleveland.

Why do you think comedians become comedians?

Because we're stupid.

What makes a joke funny?

One or more of a lot of things!

Surprise, relatability, structure, timing, silliness, truth, untruth, irony, inappropriateness, DICKS, PUSSIES, etc.

ANNE VICTORIA CLARK

🐦 *@annev6*

Anne is a stand-up comedian and writer. She is a contributor to Saturday Night Live's Weekend Update and Funny or Die's Newsflash. Originally from Omaha, Nebraska, she currently lives in New York City where she hosts two live comedy shows: Black Magic Lab Variety Show (QED) and BOMBED (Brit Pack). In the past she has contributed work to Glamour and Vanity Fair. The Toronto Standard once described her by saying that she "isn't crazy... she's smart." So that was nice.

When did you realize you were funny?

In high school I ran for sophomore class president as a joke, I was the only person who seemed to find it funny. But that was the point I realized I was very funny *to me*. I started doing improv in my early 20s and realized then that I could also make people who weren't my parents laugh, which was nice!

What did your parents do for a living when you were a kid?

They're both lawyers, which is why I'm such a nightmare to argue with :-).

What's the comedy scene like in Omaha? Did you always want to move to New York?

When I was growing up it was non-existent as far as I knew. It's blown up in the last few years though, and they have all sorts of great venues and festivals out there. As a general rule, everything gets better after I leave.

I had always wanted to move to New York, I love New York. I've lived here for a little more than eight years and I honestly can't picture myself living anywhere unless it was part of an elaborate joke.

What inspired the Royal Fetus Twitter account? What do you think it says about having good comedic timing on Twitter?

I really like parody Twitter accounts. I don't do them anymore because they jumped the shark pretty quickly. Royal Fetus was half-luck, half-obvious. I mean, their job after they got married was to have a baby, and who doesn't want to pretend to be a fetus? But yeah, I think to be funny on Twitter you have to be crazy on top of what's going on in the world.

What is writing for Weekend Update like? Can you walk me through your typical process?

I've actually never gotten a joke past dress rehearsal! Sorry! But that felt nice, so I imagine getting one on-air would feel pretty swell! I don't know that there's a process. You start with a prompt, typically a headline, and write what comes to mind. The principle of it revolves around the idea of what comes next. What crazy conclusion can you draw from the premise?

How did you first get involved?

You actually have to audition to be a contributor. It's a written one that happens once a year, they send out a packet of headlines and you have a week to return it with your best stuff!

What advice would you give someone that's trying to get published online?

Write it! Send it! Repeat! There's really no better way. 90 percent of the time when I'm not getting something published it's because I haven't written it.

How did The Lost Weekend Podcast come about? What do you enjoy most about digging through TV shows?

My friend Sean is a really insightful and funny film nut, and I enjoy talking to him about TV shows and movies. I wanted to watch the TV show Scream somewhat ironically, because I loved the movie. But I didn't want to just watch something to make fun of it. I wanted to turn it into a productive and positive experience. So I got the idea that I should watch it with Sean for analysis and invite friends around to get their takes on it as well. It ended up being a super fun way to get to know my friends better! I love getting into TV shows even if I don't love them, because it's fun to try and get inside the writer's head and try and figure out why they made each choice. That's fun to me, because I am a nerd.

What's the best thing you've seen this year and why?

I saw a movie called '71 which I put on a whim and it ended up being maybe one of the best action thrillers I'd ever seen in my life, which was pretty exciting. Crazy Ex-Girlfriend is currently my favorite TV show, because there are great jokes, lovely characters, and everyone in that cast is stupidly talented. They sing AND dance AND act! It has so much heart!

Why do you think comedians become comedians?

Because if all you can do is make jokes you're better off making a living out of it. It's a really annoying trait to just have as a person. Have you ever been trapped in a car for multiple hours with only comedians? We're horrible. We can't take anything seriously and we're always trying to be the funniest person there. Get paid for it and get it out of your system on stage so your friends and family can stop having to deal with it.

What are you working on now?

Currently I'm doing some freelance writing in branded content, desperately pitching to Weekend Update, starting a new stand-up show at The PIT in NYC in the fall, and writing a few video scripts I'm hoping to produce before the end of the year. I am also hoping to sleep at some point.

What makes a joke funny?

Just enough truth to be believed and just enough whimsy to remind you to have fun. And if you can't make that work try sarcasm.

JESUS TREJO

🐦 *@JesusTrejo*

Based out of Los Angeles, born and raised in Long Beach, Jesus has appeared on Comedy Central's "Adam Devine's House Party," Season 2 of "Stand Up and Deliver" on NuvoTV and is a recurring cast member on TBS' sitcom "Sullivan & Son." In 2015, Jesus took part in the prestigious Just For Laughs Festival in Montreal as a part of Jeff Ross' RoastMaster Invitational. Recently, Jesus had the pleasure of opening for Louie C.K. at The Comedy Store Main Room for a sold-out audience.

When did you realize you wanted to be a comedian?

I think I realized I wanted to become a comedian from a young age. My parents introduced me to Mexican comedic actors and actresses. I was just in awe of how funny they were. I really just have fond memories of watching these films with my parents.

As I grew older I came across stand-up and that was a wrap. I was enamored with the art of stand-up. I didn't really know that being a comedian was something I could pursue until I tried it in college.

What did your parents do for a living when you were a kid?

Ever since I could remember, my father was a gardener and also worked construction at a concrete company. My mother had a period of time where she was a live in maid, took care of kids, and cleaned houses. It alternated between the three for her.

Do people with full heads of hair take their locks for granted?

Hahaha! Yes, absolutely! You see so many people dyeing their hair different colors every week, not caring much for their hair. My biggest pet peeve is seeing someone with great hair decide to wear hats all the time. It's like, "What are you doing?!" I wear hats to hide my insecurities, and also to not get sun burned on the top of my head. Man, I wish I had hair...

Can you walk me through how you booked your first paid set?

I don't remember how I booked my first paid gig per say, but I do remember doing the first show I got paid at. It was a show in L.A. and the booker handed me 20 dollars (which I still have in a safe place) after the show. That felt pretty damn good. Every so often, I still pull that 20-dollar bill out and contemplate spending it when things get tough. Haha!

It seems like you have a real rapid-fire style on stage. Were you inspired by anyone in particular while you were coming up?

I think that is something I really got inspired by when I saw JB Smoove. He's a genius stand-up and improviser. I would see how he would build laughter in the room from tagging a joke over and over. JB would tag a joke to the point where you thought no more could be done and he would hit you again with a tag. That was very inspiring!

That rapid-fire style I think comes about after performing a joke over and over again, and throwing all the tags that have previously worked into it — just building over time. Seems like rapid fire, but it's essentially not having to set up another joke and ridding out the initial premise like a wave. I love that!

What's your joke-writing process? How do you come up with premises, punchlines, etc.?

I tend to start with a premise that's true to me and then I go on a journey of exaggeration, and painting a picture that makes sense to me. It's like I'm an expressionist that can convey an emotion without losing the reality. Everyone has their own way of expressing emotion, and with my comedy, things are distorted and exaggerated as a stylistic choice. I've really come to love writing and the sense of accomplishment one gets after a good writing session. I like to sit down with a premise I have tumbled in my head for the past day and try to give order to that chaotic idea on paper. I tend to write it in pencil in my little notebook, sometimes I'll type it on my phone and email it to myself. That way it's ready to go in my inbox when I decide to sit down and write.

How did you land the role of Javier on Sullivan & Son?

I'd say straight luck, haha! I met Steve Byrne while working the parking lot at The Comedy Store. I was fortunate enough to do some cool shows with Steve after that and I recall him saying to me he was going to send me an email. He said it was for an audition for a project he was working on (I knew nothing about the show at the time). I printed out a picture of me to take to the audition. I don't think I had a formal headshot or anything; I just printed it on regular paper.

I auditioned, got the call back, and tested in front of the producers, and finally I got the good news that I was cast for the part. It made me so happy to be a part of such a great show with fellow comedians and actors that I grew up watching. Surreal, blessed to have been a part of such a great show.

What was the best part of being on Adam Devine's House Party?

The best for sure had to have been being on set with all your comedian friends. Getting to eat lunch and hanging out together in another setting out side of the normal hang out was awesome.

Also making new friends with comedians I had not yet had the pleasure of working with before (it was filmed in New Orleans). I had never been before, so I was excited as heck to eat the local food and hang out in the city that is so rich in history.

You opened for Louis C.K. once at The Comedy Store. What was that night like? What makes Louie one best, if not *the* best, stand-up in the game?

I did! That night was a gift from the comedy gods. I showed up early to The Comedy Store to kill sometime before a show I had nearby. The talent coordinator (Adam) asked if I wanted to open for Louie, and I laughed out loud and obviously thought he was pulling my leg, right? What made me special that I would get offered to open Louie? I dunno… 'There are *a lot* of great comedians at the Comedy Store. Why am I getting asked?' I thought.

These were all the things that were going through my mind as I stood in the parking lot talking to my friends. Adam came back with Danny (the sound guy) and told me I would be opening and I would bring up David Spade, and Spade would bring on Louie in the Main Room. I couldn't believe this was happening. This all happened less than an hour before showtime. Talk about being at the right place and right time!

Louie is definitely one of the best in the world because he had to work at it. He's been in the game for a long time, and it wasn't until a long time of grinding on the road and hustling that he became the 'Louie' we all know and love today. He's a prime example of the type of career we as comedians hope we're blessed to have one day. A career with longevity comes about by not taking any shortcuts. It's math— our careers in comedy are best represented by a bell curve with the first half being mirrors to the second half of the bell curve.

However long it took you to get to the peak of the wave, that will be very indicative to how long it takes for you to go back down (and repeat the cycle again hopefully). His work ethic must be INSANE, given his awesome ever-expanding library, and the quantity of content he's able to put out year after year.

Why do you think comedians become comedians?

I think there is a void in most comedians. I don't know what that may be but there is something comedians are searching for to fill that void. Comedians are not normal people. We're all misfits, it seems to me. I wish I could remember who told me this, but they said something along the lines of "Comedians don't choose to become comedians— comedy chooses them." I thought that was such a dope way of looking at it. But I guess that initial spark is triggered by someone telling them, "Hey, you're funny!" and she or he decides to explore that side of themselves.

Once, I guess, *comedy chooses you* and you've decided this is what you're going to do with your life, it becomes a never ending pursuit of being a comedian. I recall reading that we all have an idea of what a comedian is, and as comedians, we go up there and do an impression of the comedian we think we're supposed to be. This is often not as funny as the person offstage making his or her friends laugh. I'm guilty of this too. If only I could be as funny as I am around my friends on stage! I would be set, haha!

To me I think a comedian becomes a comedian because they've accepted the challenge of trying to bring on stage the person they are off stage.

What makes a joke funny?

This consists of lots of variables.

The premise—is it based in reality? If it is, the joke would likely be more relatable to people and the human experience and people will be on-board. Is there misdirection? Meaning, did it come to a conclusion that you did not see coming? The purpose of the punch line is really just releasing the tension the set-up built in the beginning. The delivery of the joke is also very important.

How many of my jokes have been lost in the delivery of a well-crafted joke on paper? (Too many times for me to count.) Having the audience on-board with your window of reference is good, too. I hate when people don't understand a comedians joke and their first response is: "I don't think he was funny at all!" This sucks, and brings me to my last point: comedy is subjective.

What you think is funny may or may not be funny to you or the person next to you. All of this is me really trying to make sense of what makes a joke funny. What do I know?

ABOUT THE AUTHOR

Zuri is a writer born and raised in Los Angeles.

He spent two years in Kenya as a child and four years in Syracuse as a larger child. Today he works as a web editor. This is his first book and he really hopes you like it.

Special thanks to: Ms. Moody, Dr. Draper, Prof. Burton, Randall, Donna, Nick Balsamo, Danny Tabor, William Turner, Julia Gillespie, Tony Olivero, Brett LoGiurato, Paris Peckerman, Curtis Greene and Mark Potter (the funniest people I know).